I0490306

ART BOOKS

FROM CRESCENT MOON PUBLISHING

Leonardo da Vinci
by James Pearson

Early Netherlandish Painting
by Rosalind Mutter

Piero della Francesca
by Naomi Haskell

Giovanni Bellini
by Julia Davis

Eric Gill: Nuptials of God
by Anthony Hoyland

Minimal Art and Artists In the 1960s and After
by Laura Garrard

Postwar Art
by George Knighton

Vincent van Gogh: Visionary Landscapes
by Stuart Morris

Max Beckmann
by Stuart Morris

Egon Schiele: Sex and Death in Purple Stockings
by D. Simon Eade

Mark Rothko: The Art of Transcendence
by Julia Davis

Jasper Johns
by L.M. Poole

Brice Marden
by Laura Garrard

Frank Stella: American Abstract Artist
by James Pearson

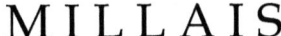

MILLAIS

MILLAIS

BY A. LYS BALDRY

CRESCENT MOON

First published 1912. This edition © 2020.

Set in Book Antiqua 10 on 14pt.
Designed by Radiance Graphics.

British Library Cataloguing in Publication data

ISBN-13 9781861716507

CRESCENT MOON PUBLISHING
P.O. Box 1312, Maidstone, Kent, ME14 5XU
Great Britain, www.crmoon.com

CONTENTS

NOTE ON THE TEXT

The text is from *Millais* by A. Lys Baldry, and published by Frederick A. Stokes Company, New York, 1899/ 1912.

The illustrations in the original text are included in the illustrations section, along with many other works.

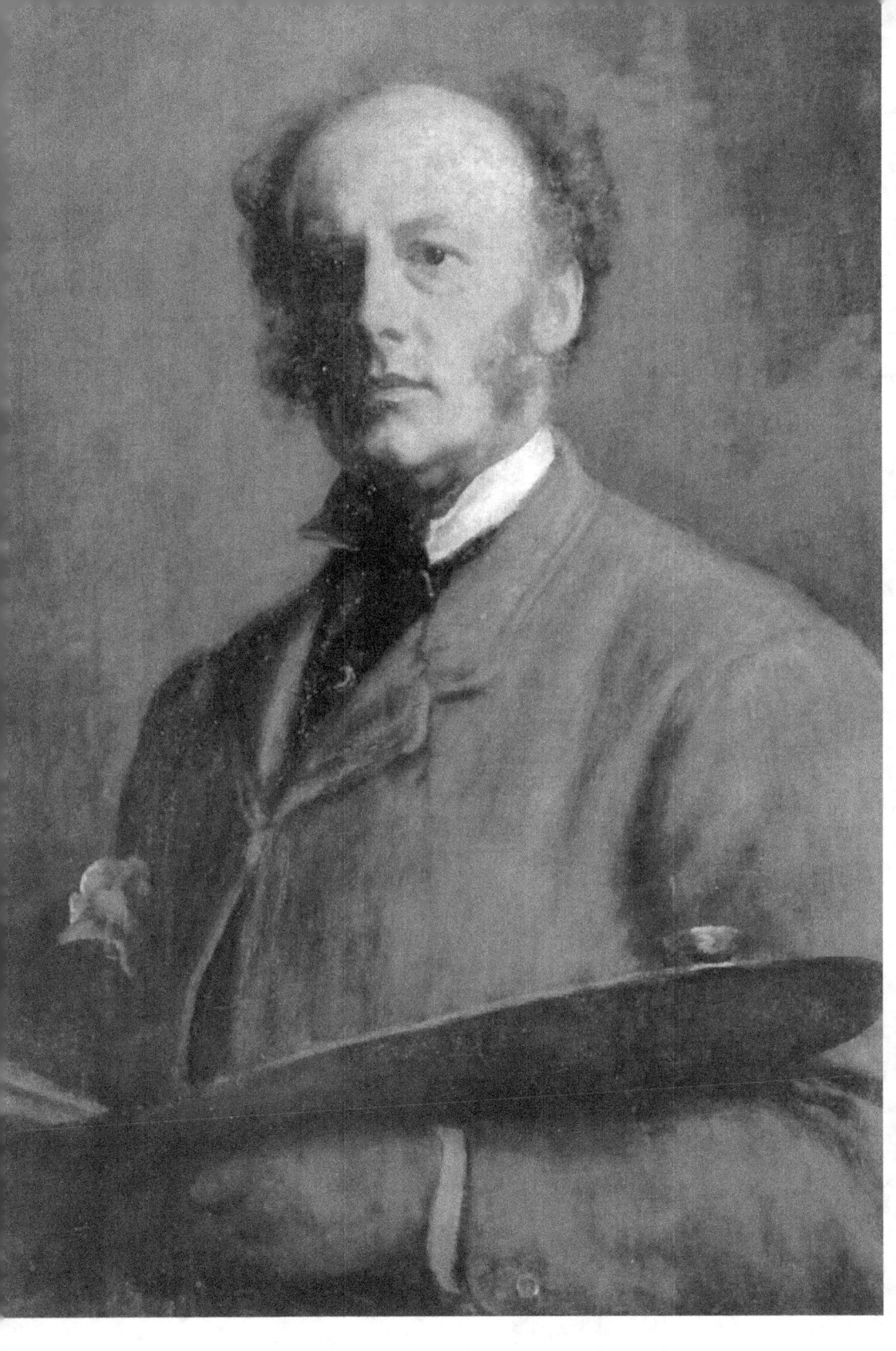

John Everett Millais, Self-Portrait, 1881, Uffizi, Florence

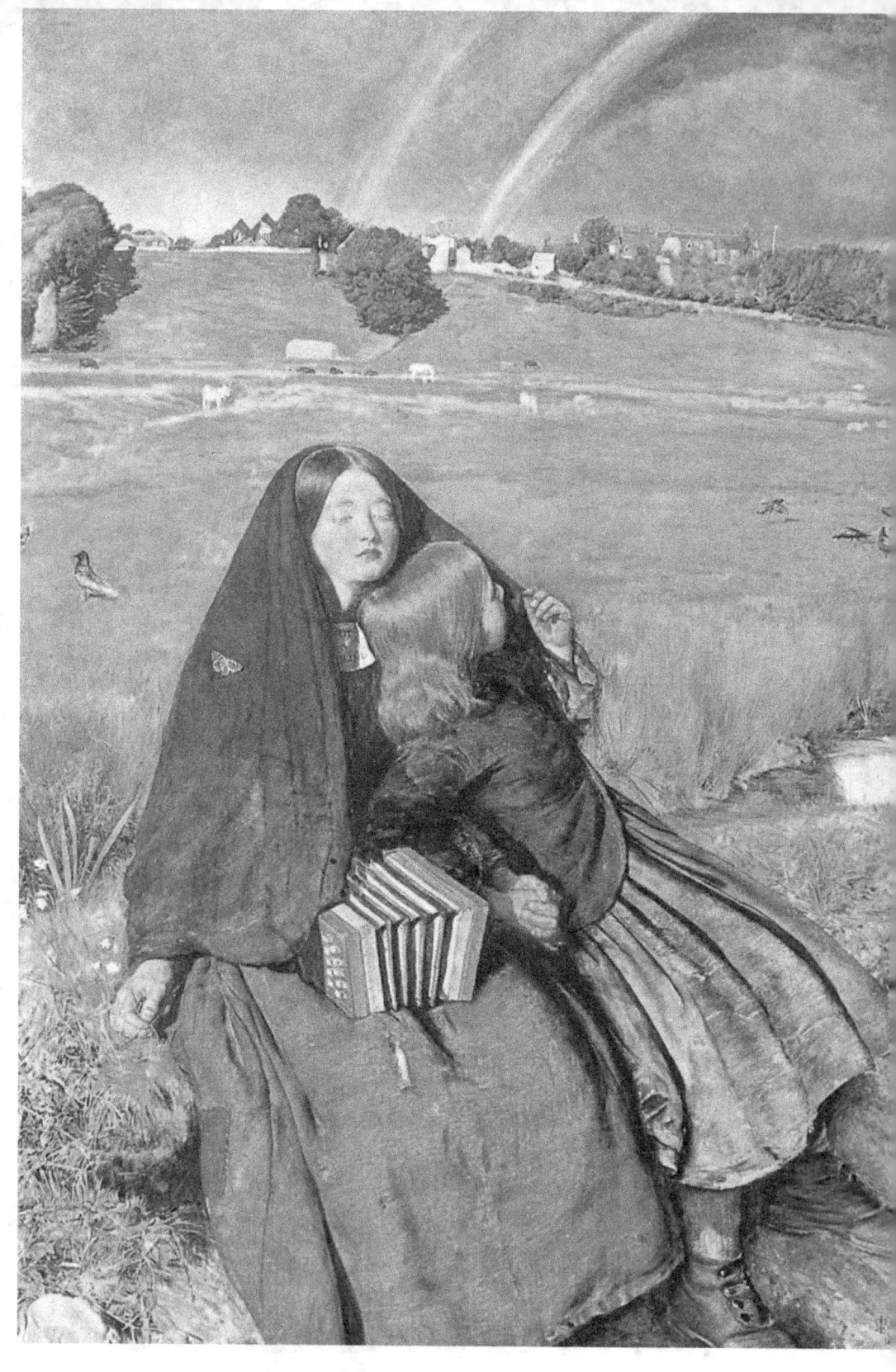

John Everett Millais, Blind Girl, 1885, Birmingham

MILLAIS

As a record of some half century of brilliant activity, and of practically unbroken success, the life-story of John Everett Millais is in many respects unlike those which can be told about the majority of artists who have played great parts in the modern art world. He had none of the hard struggle for recognition, or of the fight against adverse circumstances, which have too often embittered the earlier years of men destined to take eventually the highest rank in their profession. Things went well with him from the first; he gained attention at an age when most painters have barely begun to make a bid for popularity, and his position was assured almost before he had arrived at man's estate. He owed some of his success, no doubt, to his attractive and vigorous personality, but it was due in far greater measure to the extraordinary powers which he manifested from the very outset of his career.

For there was something almost sensational in the manner of his development, in his unusual precocity, and in the youthful self-confidence which enabled him to take a prominent place among the leaders of artistic opinion while he was still little more than a boy. So early was the proof given that he possessed absolutely uncommon powers, that he was not more than nine years old when he began serious art training; and so evident even then was his destiny that this training was commenced on the advice of Sir Martin Archer Shee, the President of the Royal Academy, to whom the child's performances had been submitted by parents anxious for an expert opinion. The President's declaration when he saw these early efforts, that "nature had provided for the boy's success," was emphatic enough to dissipate any doubts there might have been whether or not young Millais was to be encouraged in his artistic inclinations; and that this emphasis was justified by subsequent results no one to-day can dispute.

The family from which Millais sprang was not one with any past record of art achievement. His ancestors were men of action and inclined rather to be fighters than students of the arts. They were Normans who had settled in Jersey, and had for several hundred years been counted among the more important landholders in that island, where at different times they held several estates. From these ancestors Millais derived his energetic temperament and that militant activity which enabled him in his career as an artist to triumph signally over established prejudices – the qualities which undoubtedly helped him to make his power felt even by the people who were most opposed to him.

He was born on June 8th, 1829, at Southampton, where his parents were temporarily living, but his earliest years were spent in Jersey. It was in 1835 that he began to show definitely his artistic inclinations; he was at Dinan then with his parents and he amused himself there by making sketches of the country and people with success so remarkable that even strangers did not hesitate to recognise him as a budding genius. Three years later this estimate was confirmed by Sir Martin Archer Shee, and the boy was then sent to work at the art school which Henry Sass carried on in Bloomsbury, a school which had at that time a considerable reputation as a training place for art students, and in which most of the early Victorian painters received their preliminary education.

Soon after he entered this school Millais gave a very striking proof of his precocious ability – he gained the silver medal of the

Society of Arts for a drawing of the antique, and an amusing story is told of the sensation he created when he appeared at the prize-giving to receive his award. The Duke of Sussex was presiding at the meeting, and to his amazement, when the name of "Mr Millais" was called, a small child presented himself as the winner of the medal. To amazement succeeded admiration when a consultation with the officials of the Society proved that this boy of nine was really the successful competitor, and the presentation was received with great applause by the spectators of the scene.

After two years' work under Sass, with some study in the British Museum in addition, he was admitted into the schools of the Royal Academy, and, though his age then was only eleven, he began almost immediately to prove how well he could hold his own in this new sphere of activity. During the six years over which his studentship at the Academy extended he won every prize for which he competed, and carried off finally the gold medal for historical painting with a picture of "The Tribe of Benjamin Seizing the Daughters of Shiloh." This was in 1847; in the previous year he had made his first appearance as an exhibitor at the Academy with an ambitious composition, "Pizarro Seizing the Inca of Peru," which is now in the Victoria and Albert Museum. His most ambitious effort at this period was, however, the design, "The Widow Bestowing her Mite," which he produced in 1847 for the Westminster Hall competition, a vast canvas crowded with life-sized figures which was remarkable enough to have made the reputation of a far older and more experienced painter.

So far his progress had been without interruption. The rare brilliancy of his student career had gained him the fullest approval of his fellow-workers in art, and he was beginning his career as a producer with every prospect of becoming immediately one of the most popular artists of his time. Everything was in his favour; he had undeniable ability, good health, and an attractive personality, and he had proved in many ways that, young as he was, he could handle large undertakings with sound judgment and complete confidence. Yet, with what seemed to be his way smooth before him, he did not hesitate to risk his already assured position in the art world by setting himself openly in opposition to the opinions of practically all the men who were then counted as the leaders of his profession. That he knew what might be the penalty he would have to pay for this rebellion against the fashion of the moment can scarcely be doubted, but he was by nature too strenuous a fighter to be daunted by dangerous possibilities, and his convictions, once formed, were always too strong to yield to any considerations of expediency.

In 1848, he and two friends of about his own age, Dante Gabriel Rossetti, and William Holman Hunt, conceived the idea of making a practical protest against the inefficiency of the work which was being done by the more popular artists of the time. The three youths had come under the influence of Ford Madox Brown, who with splendid sincerity was labouring to realise an ideal based not upon fashion, but upon an earnest desire for truthful expression, and by his example they were induced to study a purer type of art than any they could see about them. For this purer art they turned to the works of the Italian Primitives, whose childlike unconventionality and unhesitating naturalism touched a responsive chord in the natures of these youths who still retained some of the simple faith in reality which is one of the charms of childhood. They decided that for the future they would base their own practice upon that of the early Italians, and that they would have none of the artificialities of the age in which they found themselves. Their resolve was a bold one, but the manner in which they proceeded to make it effective was bolder still.

They organised an association, the title of which, "The Pre-Raphaelite Brotherhood," significantly asserted the nature of their artistic aims, and as the founders of this association they pledged themselves to seek the inspiration of their art in those Italian painters who had lived before Raphael was born, and whose sterling principles were abandoned by Raphael and his successors. To the three founders of the Brotherhood were joined two other painters, James Collinson, and F.G. Stephens, a sculptor, Thomas Woolner and Dante Gabriel Rossetti's brother, William Michael, who, being a writer, was given the office of secretary. The Brotherhood, so constituted, was formally inaugurated in the autumn of 1848, and the members at once set to work to prove by their acts the reality of their belief in the creed they had adopted.

The first fruits of the movement were seen in the following spring at the Academy where Millais, who was then, it must be remembered, not quite twenty, exhibited his "Lorenzo and Isabella," a picture striking in its originality and in its unusual power. What it implied was not, however, immediately realised by the public; that the manner of the painting made it very unlike those by which it was surrounded was generally recognised, but most people, if they thought about the matter at all, seem to have assumed that the painter had failed to bring himself into line with the art of his time through youthful inexperience rather than by deliberate intention. Time and practice, they considered, would correct such deficiencies in taste as were apparent in the "Lorenzo and Isabella," and when the lad had arrived at years of discretion he would be the first to see the necessity for amendment.

But the members of the Brotherhood, probably feeling that their initial effort had not produced quite the effect intended, took other steps to define their attitude. They started, in January 1850, a magazine called *The Germ*, which was proffered as the organ of the new movement. It was sufficiently uncompromising in its confession of faith, and neither its text nor its illustrations were wanting in clearness of statement. The magazine, indeed, was what it was intended to be, an open challenge to all the advocates of the old order of things; and as such it was taken by the people who saw it. It was only in existence for four months, but even in that short time it did its work thoroughly, and put an end to any doubts there were in the minds of art lovers and art workers concerning the meaning of Pre-Raphaelitism; thenceforward Millais and his friends had certainly no reason to complain of being ignored.

The attention which was given to the pictures they sent to the 1850 Academy exhibition was, however, by no means what they desired, though, doubtless, it must have been much what they expected. Millais exhibited a "Portrait of a Gentleman and his Grandchild," "Ferdinand Lured by Ariel," and "Christ in the House of His Parents" – better known as "The Carpenter's Shop" – and these visible embodiments of the principles laid down in *The Germ* were received with an absolute storm of abuse. The audacity of the young painters who sought by works of this character to discredit the smug and artificial respectability of the art which was then in vogue excited the critics beyond control and brought forth a veritable orgie of virulent expostulation.

Millais, with his mind made up and his fighting instinct fully roused, was not the man to yield to clamour. He made no concessions, but, loyally supporting the policy of the Brotherhood, showed at the Academy in 1851 "The Woodman's Daughter," "Mariana in the Moated Grange," and "The Return of the Dove to the Ark," all of which were as frank in their Pre-Raphaelitism as any of the previous year's canvases, and all of which were greeted with even more vehement disapproval by the literary custodians of the popular taste. Every possible kind of misrepresentation of the aims of the young painter and his friends was employed to discredit their efforts, all sorts of base motives were imputed to them; ridicule, specious argument, and insult were used in turn to drive them from the course they had deliberately chosen. Appeals were even made to the Academy to have the pictures, round which this controversy was raging, removed summarily from the exhibition as things unfit to be set before the eyes of the public. But fortunately the courage of the Brotherhood was proof against everything which the opposition could do, and neither abuse nor threats had any effect. Yet Millais at the time suffered for his principles; paintings which had been commissioned were thrown upon his hands, and his pictures almost ceased to be saleable. He had every proof that his Pre-Raphaelitism was commercially a mistake and that, if he persisted, the absolute marring of his career as a popular painter, was more than likely, yet, so stubborn was his conviction that he made no change in either his principles or his practice.

Happily, as time went on, the position of affairs began to improve; the opposition exhausted itself by excess of violence, and able champions of the movement took up the cudgels in defence of the young artists. One of the most authoritative of these champions was Ruskin, who found in this apparently forlorn hope infinite possibilities of artistic progress, and whose declaration that the Pre-Raphaelites were laying "the foundations of a school of art nobler than the world has seen for three hundred years" generously expressed his sentiments towards the Brotherhood. He took the trouble to study their art, and to analyse their motives, so that he based his advocacy not upon vague sympathy but upon real understanding of artistic principles which were sane and sound enough to satisfy even his exacting demand for purity of æsthetic purpose. That the ultimate success of Pre-Raphaelitism was due to his energetic interposition cannot, of course, be claimed – the boldness and tenacity of the artists who had adopted the new creed had more to do with the improvement which was brought about in the popular attitude – but Ruskin's counter attack upon the critics had a valuable effect, and undoubtedly helped greatly to open the eyes of the public.

It is interesting, too, to note that just at the moment when the attack was fiercest the Royal Academy showed its faith in Millais by electing him an Associate. He is said to have been the youngest student ever received into the Academy schools, and he must have been one of the youngest painters ever chosen as an Associate, for after his election it was discovered that he had not reached the age at which, under the Academy rules, admission to the Associateship was possible. So his election had to be declared invalid and he had to wait some few years longer – until 1853 –

for the official recognition of his claims. But it must assuredly be counted to the credit of the Academy that such readiness should have been shown to admit the ability of a young artist who was openly in rebellion against the fashions of his time, and whose work was by implication a condemnation of much that was being done even by members of the Academic circle.

His election in 1853 came more as a matter of course; by that date he had won his way to a position which could scarcely be questioned even by the bitterest opponents of Pre-Raphaelitism, and he had laid securely the foundations of that remarkable popularity which he was destined to enjoy for the rest of his life. It would have been hard, indeed, to deny that he deserved whatever rewards were due to artistic merit of the highest order, for his pictures had passed well beyond the stage of brilliant promise into that of commanding achievement. His "Ophelia" and "The Huguenot" in 1852, his "Order of Release" and "The Proscribed Royalist" in 1853, and his exquisite "Portrait of Mr. Ruskin" in 1854, are to be accounted as masterly performances which would have done full credit to a painter whose skill had been matured by more than half a lifetime of strenuous effort, and which, as the productions of a young man who did not reach his twenty-fifth birthday until the summer of 1854, are of really extraordinary importance. The "Ophelia," "The Huguenot," and "The Order of Release," can be placed, indeed, among the most memorable expositions of his artistic conviction, and the "Portrait of Mr. Ruskin" ranks with the "Ophelia" as one of the most astonishing examples of searching and faithful study which can be found in modern art.

These pictures were followed closely by others not less notable – by "The Rescue" in 1855, by "Autumn Leaves," "The Random Shot," "The Blind Girl," and "Peace Concluded," in 1856, and by "Sir Isumbras at the Ford," "The Escape of a Heretic," and "News from Home," in 1857. Of this group "Sir Isumbras at the Ford" was the least successful, but "Autumn Leaves," with its exquisite delicacy of sentiment, and those two delightful little canvases,

"The Blind Girl," and "The Random Shot," are of supreme interest both on account of the depth of thought which they reveal and of their splendid executive accomplishment.

Another great picture appeared in 1859 – "The Vale of Rest," which differed from most of the works which Millais had hitherto produced in its larger qualities of handling and more serious symbolism. Its special importance was not fully realised by the artist's admirers when it was first exhibited, but Millais himself looked upon it as the best thing he had done; and this opinion has since been generally recognised as sufficiently well founded. He had not before shown so much solemnity of feeling nor quite so complete a grasp of the larger pictorial essentials, though in "Autumn Leaves" there was decidedly more than a hint of the seriousness of purpose which gave authority and dignity of style to "The Vale of Rest."

There was at this time a change coming over his art, a change which suggested that the stricter limits of Pre-Raphaelitism were a little too narrow for him now that his youthful enthusiasms were being replaced by the more tolerant ideas of mental maturity. But he was in no haste to abandon his earlier principles; he sought rather to find how they might be widened to cover artistic motives which scarcely came within the scope of the creed to which the Brotherhood had originally been pledged. So he alternated between the literalism of "The Black Brunswicker" (1860), "The White Cockade" (1862), "My First Sermon" (1863), "My Second Sermon" (1864), and "Asleep" and "Awake," which were shown in 1867 with that daintiest of all his earlier paintings, "The Minuet," and the sombre suggestion of such imaginative pictures as "The Enemy Sowing Tares," and the finely conceived "Eve of St. Agnes," of which the former was exhibited at the Academy in 1865, and the latter in 1863. It seemed as if he was trying to make up his mind as to the direction he was to take for the future, testing his powers in various ways, and studying himself to see how his wishes and his temperament could best be brought into accord.

But when in 1868 he broke into the new art world in which he was to reign supreme for nearly thirty years, his abandonment of the technical methods which he had adopted in 1849, and used ever since with comparatively little modification, was as decisive as it was surprising. In 1867 he was the careful, searching, and literal student of small details, precise in brushwork, and exactly realistic in his record of what he had microscopically examined. His "Asleep" and "Awake" were in his most matter-of-fact vein, almost pedantically accurate in statement of obvious facts; and even his charming "Minuet" was elaborated with a care that left nothing for the imagination to supply. In 1868, however, all this dwelling upon little things, all this studied minuteness of touch and literal presentation of what was obvious, had suddenly disappeared. All that remained to him of his Pre-Raphaelitism was the acuteness of vision which had served him so well for twenty years in his intimate examination of nature; everything else had gone, his minute actuality was replaced by large and generous suggestion, his restrained brushwork by the broadest and most emphatic handling, his realistic view by a kind of magnificent impressionism which expressed rightly enough the personal robustness of the man himself.

What made this change the more dramatic was the absence of any suggestion in his previous work that he was preparing for an executive departure of such a marked kind. A diversion into a new class of subjects, or an inclination towards a more serious type of sentiment, might perhaps have been looked for from the painter of "The Vale of Rest," "The Enemy Sowing Tares," and "The Eve of St. Agnes," but even in the larger manner of these pictures, there was little to imply that he desired to adopt a new mode of painting. But if the "Souvenir of Velazquez," "Stella," "The Pilgrims to St. Paul's," and "The Sisters," which he contributed to the 1868 Academy, are compared with what he had done before, the full significance of his action can be perceived.

The "Souvenir of Velazquez," indeed, is one of the most decisive pieces of fluent brushwork which has been produced by any modern painter of the British school. It is entirely convincing in its directness and in its summariness of executive suggestion, and as a masterly performance it is by no means unworthy to stand beside the works of that master to whom it was in some sort designed as a tribute. But it has a peculiarly English charm which Millais grafted with happy discretion on to the technical manner of the Spanish school, and as a study of childish grace it is almost inimitably persuasive. The little princesses whom Velazquez painted were too often robbed of their daintiness by the formality of the surroundings in which it was their misfortune to be placed, but the child in this picture by Millais has lost none of her freshness, and, with all her finery, is still a happy, young, little thing, ready for a romp as soon as the sitting is over. In the long series of fascinating studies of child-life which he painted with quite exquisite sympathy, this one claims a place of particular prominence on account of its beauty of characterisation, and its entire absence of affectation, quite as much as it does on account of its qualities as a consummate exercise in craftsmanship.

This was the canvas which he finally decided to hand over to the Academy as his diploma work. He had been promoted to the rank of Academician in 1863, and his intention then was to be represented in the Diploma Gallery by "The Enemy Sowing Tares," which he regarded as in every way a sound example of his powers. But his fellow-Academicians, for some not very intelligible reason, did not agree with him about the suitability of this picture, and it was, therefore, refused. So he sent them the "Souvenir of Velazquez" instead, a fortunate choice, for it brought permanently into a quasi-public gallery what is indisputably an achievement worthy of him at his best.

Once started on his new direction as a painter he went forward with unhesitating confidence in his ability to realise his intentions, and as the years passed by he added picture after picture to the already large company of his successes. His admirers, surprised as they were at first by his startling change of manner, did not hesitate to accept what he had to offer; indeed the splendid vigour of his work brought him an immediate increase of popularity, and he was thenceforth recognised at home and abroad as one of the most commanding figures in the whole array of British art, as a leader whose authority was not to be questioned.

In 1869 he exhibited his portrait of "Nina, Daughter of F. Lehmann, Esq.," "The Gambler's Wife," a "Portrait of Sir John Fowler," and "Vanessa," a companion picture to his "Stella;" and in 1870 "A Widow's Mite," "The Boyhood of Raleigh," and "The Knight Errant," with some other works of less importance. The portrait of Miss Lehmann is one of the pictures upon which his reputation most securely rests, admirable in its technical quality and its observation of character; and among the others "The Boyhood of Raleigh," and "The Knight Errant," are worthiest of attention because they are treated with great distinction, and have in large measure that interest which always results from judicious interpretation of a well-selected subject.

"The Boyhood of Raleigh," especially, is to be considered on account of its possession of a certain dramatic sentiment which might easily have been made theatrical by an artist less surely endowed with a sense of fitness. But it tells its story with charm and conviction, and there is in the action of the figures, and in the expressions on the faces, just the right degree of vitality needed to make clear the pictorial motive. "The Knight Errant" is, perhaps, less significant as a piece of invention, but it has a distinct place in the artist's list of achievements, because it affords one of the few instances of his treatment of the nude figure on a large scale. It proves plainly enough that his avoidance of subjects of this class was not due to any inability on his part to succeed as a flesh painter, for this figure is beautiful both in colour and handling; it is more probable that the classic formality and conventionality which public opinion in this country requires in the representation of the nude did not appeal to a man with his love of actuality and sincere regard for nature's facts. Indeed, from the standpoint of the decorative figure painter – of men like Leighton, or Albert Moore, for instance – the woman that Millais has represented is too frankly unidealised, too modern in type, and too realistically feminine.

But in this disregard of convention there is a kind of summing up of his beliefs as an artist. Though he had changed the outward aspect of his art he was still in spirit a Pre-Raphaelite, and a Pre-Raphaelite he remained to the end of his days. He depended more upon the keenness of vision natural to him, and assiduously cultivated by years of close observation, than upon what powers he may have had of abstract imagining; and he sought to only a limited extent to set down upon his canvas those mental images which satisfy men who look upon nature chiefly as a basis for decorative designs. The mental image with him was a direct reflection of fact, not an adaptation modified and formalised in accordance with recognised rules, not a fancy more or less remotely referable to reality; but he had certainly an ample equipment of that taste which enables the painter to discriminate between the realities which are too crude and obvious to be worth recording, and those which by their inherent beauty claim a permanent place in an artist's memory. He had, too, the judgment to see that the nude, treated as it would have to be to satisfy his æsthetic conscience, would be too plainly stated to be entirely acceptable.

He found a much more appropriate field for the exercise of his particular capacities by turning to landscape painting. Many of his earlier figure compositions had been given backgrounds which showed how well he could manage the complex details of masses of tangled vegetation, or the broad and simple lines of a piece of rural scenery; but in 1871 he attempted for the first time a landscape which was complete in itself and not merely incidental in a picture mainly concerned with human interest. This landscape, "Chill October," was at the Academy with his "Yes or No?" "Victory, O Lord," "A Somnambulist," and the "Portrait of George Grote," and it was welcomed by a host of admirers as a new revelation of his versatility. It has certainly qualities which justify the estimation in which it was and is still held; and though it lacks that imaginative insight into poetic subtleties which accounts for so much in the work of a master like Turner, it must always claim the respect of art lovers as a large, dignified, and sincere study of nature in one of her sadder moods. It is the reserve of the picture, its reticent realism, that chiefly makes it memorable, for it is neither imposing in subject nor striking in effect; but in its broad simplicity there is something rarely fascinating.

Other nature studies of the same character followed at brief intervals during the next few years; they added to the interest of the artist's practice, but they can scarcely be said to have equalled in importance the portraits and figure subjects which he completed at this stage of his career. Millais was, of course, far too great a master to have failed in any branch of artistic practice to which he seriously devoted himself, but the very capacities which made him so successful as a painter of the human subject prevented him from looking at open-air nature with the necessary degree of abstraction. The physical character of a piece of scenery, its details and individual peculiarities, he could record with absolute certainty, though the elusive subtleties of atmosphere, and the charming accidents of illumination, which mean so much in the poetic rendering of landscape, he dwelt upon hardly at all. In many of his landscapes the breadth and dignity, the accurate relation of part to part, the fascinating simplicity of manner, which are among the greater merits of "Chill October," can be praised without reservation or hesitation; but the touch of fantasy, of actual unreality, by which the inspired landscape painter seems to suggest more truly the real spirit of nature, he hardly ever attempted; and never, it may fairly be said, with complete success.

The years over which his activity as an exponent of pure landscape extended are, however, memorable because they saw the production of some of the most triumphant achievements of his maturer life. With his two landscapes, "Flowing to the Sea," and "Flowing to the River," he exhibited in 1872 his "Hearts are Trumps," a portrait group which has become a modern classic; and in 1873 another wonderful portrait, the three-quarter length of "Mrs. Bischoffsheim." But it was in 1874 that he showed what is in many ways the greatest of all his paintings, "The North-West Passage," a work which, if he had done nothing else of moment, would suffice to place him securely among the master painters of the world. The head of the old man, who is the central figure in the picture, is entirely magnificent, and there is much besides in this canvas which would have been beyond the reach of any one but an artist of almost abnormal power. This was followed in 1875 by his portrait of "Miss Eveleen Tennant," and in 1877 by the "Yeoman of the Guard," which runs "The North-West Passage" close in the race for supremacy.

At this time, indeed, his productiveness was extraordinary; subject pictures, portraits, and landscapes appeared in rapid succession, and in all of them he kept to a level of masterly practice which other men reach only occasionally and at rare intervals. Between 1873 and 1879 he painted eight landscapes, all important in scale and interesting in treatment, but after 1879 he produced no more for nearly ten years, when he began a fresh series. He was apparently too busy with portraits and figure subjects to give much time to out-of-door work, and to satisfy the demands made upon him by art collectors and sitters he must have had to work his hardest. Yet popularity did not make him careless, and his hard work diminished neither his freshness of outlook nor his freedom of expression. Conscientiousness as a craftsman was always one of his virtues, and the knowledge that he had a host of admirers ready to accept almost anything he would give them had certainly not the effect of inducing him to lower his standard.

In the long list of his paintings, which belong to the period beginning in 1879 and ending in 1888, several stand out with special prominence – for example, his portraits of "Mrs. Jopling," and "The Right Hon. W. E. Gladstone," "Cherry Ripe," and "The

Princess Elizabeth," all in 1879, "The Right Hon. John Bright" in 1880, "Cardinal Newman," "Alfred, Lord Tennyson," "Sir Henry Thompson," "Cinderella," and "Caller Herrin'," in 1881, "J. C. Hook, R.A.," and "The Captive," in 1882, "The Marquess of Salisbury" in 1883, "The Ruling Passion," and another portrait of Gladstone, in 1885, "Bubbles" in 1886, and "The Marquess of Hartington" in 1887. Some of these were shown at the Academy, but he was producing far more year by year than could be exhibited there, so he sent many important works to the Grosvenor Gallery, and most of his subject pictures to the galleries of the dealers by whom they were commissioned.

After 1888 there was some relaxation in his effort; in that year he had at the Academy only one picture, a landscape, "Murthly Moss," and only one portrait in each of the years 1889 and 1890, though he showed several works in other galleries. In 1892 his landscapes "Halcyon Weather," and "Blow, Blow, thou Winter Wind," were at the Academy, but after that year he worked no more out-of-doors. Of the canvases painted during the last three or four years of his life, the most memorable are his portrait of "John Hare" (1893), "Speak! Speak!" (1895), and "A Forerunner" (1896), all of which were at the Academy, and "Time the Reaper" which was at the New Gallery in 1895. "Speak! Speak!" was purchased by the Chantrey Fund trustees, and is now in the National Gallery of British Art with the other admirably chosen examples of his art which were given to the nation by Sir Henry Tate.

The crowning honour of his life came to him in February 1896, when he was elected President of the Royal Academy in succession to Lord Leighton – an honour which was particularly appropriate not only because of his eminence as an artist, but also because he had been intimately connected for nearly sixty years with the institution over which he was then called to preside. To this connection he referred in his speech at the Academy banquet in 1895, at which he took the chair in the place of Leighton whose illness prevented him from occupying his accustomed position. The words which Millais used on this occasion expressed generously and affectionately his sense of obligation to the Academy by which he had been trained in his boyhood, and from which he had received encouragement and support at the most critical period of his career, and declared with characteristic frankness that he owed to it a debt of gratitude which he never could repay.

To those, however, who know how loyal he was to the institution that he loved so well it would seem that the debt was, indeed, fully paid. Few men have done more to uphold the repute of the Academy, few have by the brilliancy of their powers and their charm of personality done it more credit. That Leighton was the ideal President can be readily admitted, but Millais, as his successor, would have carried on a great tradition with dignity and sympathy and with no diminution of his predecessor's generous tolerance and earnest sense of artistic responsibility. He would have kept the Academy on broad lines, and by his impatience of empty formalities he would have prevented it from losing touch with the movements in modern art.

But, unfortunately, he was destined to hold his honourable office for but a brief time. Even before Leighton's death he had been suffering from a throat trouble which not long after was pronounced to be cancer; and in the months that followed immediately on his election the disease made rapid progress. Not long after the opening of the 1896 Academy Exhibition his condition became so serious that an immediately fatal result was expected; but by an operation he obtained some temporary relief and his life was prolonged for a few weeks. This, however, was only a brief respite; he died on August 13, and was buried a week later in St. Paul's Cathedral, where little more than six months before he had followed his old friend's body to the grave.

To speak of his death as premature would be scarcely a misapplication of the word. Although Millais had completed his sixty-seventh year he was still in art a young man. His vigour had not waned, and there was no perceptible diminution of his artistic vitality even in those last works which he painted under the shadow of nearly impending death. To a man of his splendid physique and buoyant temperament age would have come slowly, and the inevitable degeneration of his powers would have not begun for many more years. The possibility of great achievement remained to him, and it would be true to say that his death robbed us of much which would have added greatly to the sum total of British art. Yet we may be grateful to fate for allowing him to develop the promise of his youth in the splendour of his maturer years; it is so often the lot of the precocious genius to die young with his mission but half fulfilled. If death had come to Millais as it did to Bonington or Fred Walker, our loss would have been sad indeed.

In discussing Millais as an artist the part which his personality played in making him what he was must by no means be overlooked. Something of the vitality and the virility of his art was due to the way in which he kept touch with the life about him, and interested himself in people and things. He was no recluse who fed in secret upon his own ideas, or narrowed his outlook by hedging himself round with prejudices and preferences for one special class of artistic material. Instead, he went out into the world and acquired his impressions of humanity in all directions and at first hand, finding much pleasure in association with his fellow-men. To his own human nature he gave free rein; he was a keen sportsman, a lover of children – of whose ways he had, as he proved in scores of pictures, a perfect understanding – and a man who was always happy in congenial society, and always welcome. He lived his life, in fact, largely, genially, and wholesomely, and he was as much unspoiled by the prosperity which came to him in his maturer years as he was unshaken by the opposition which he had to face in that brief period of his youth when, as he used to say himself, he was "so dreadfully bullied."

That this brief taste of unpopularity did him good rather than harm can well be imagined, for without making him bitter it tested with some severity his tenacity and his power to fight vigorously for what he believed to be right – and such a test has always its value as a means of developing the finer qualities of a strong man, or as a warning to the weak one of the need for self-examination. Millais did not require any incentive to self-examination, because he knew well enough what he intended to do when he deliberately set up his own conviction against that of the men who practically ruled British art, and he did not enter upon the fight with any idea of backing out if he found it was likely to go against him. But after the kind of triumphal progress which he made through the Academy schools, the discovery that the wider public was not disposed to accept him as infallible was possibly necessary to prove to him that successes as a student did not give him, as a matter of course, an assured place among the chiefs of his profession. He was taught roughly, and in a way that roused both his fighting spirit and his pride, that this position was to be won only by sustained and strenuous effort; and this lesson he never forgot. Its effects persisted long after he had become a popular favourite, and they helped, it can be fairly believed, to strengthen his character and to keep him from that easy contentment with his own works which is the first step towards degeneration. He did not degenerate after he had secured what he had been striving for; although he had silenced his critics, and had won them over to his side, he continued to sit in severest judgment upon himself, and to the last he exacted from his own capacities the utmost they could give him.

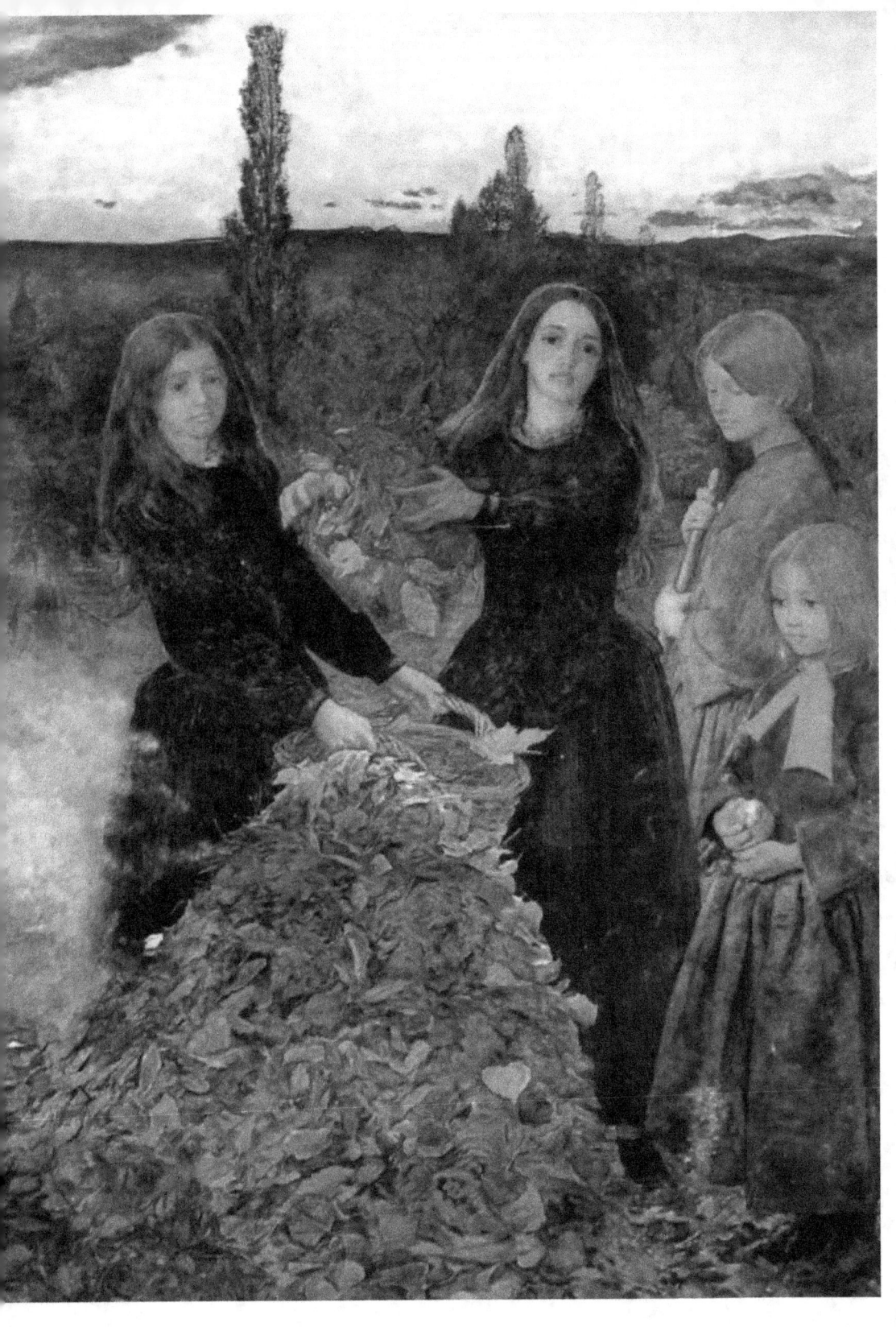

John Everett Millais, Autumn Leaves, 1856, Manchester

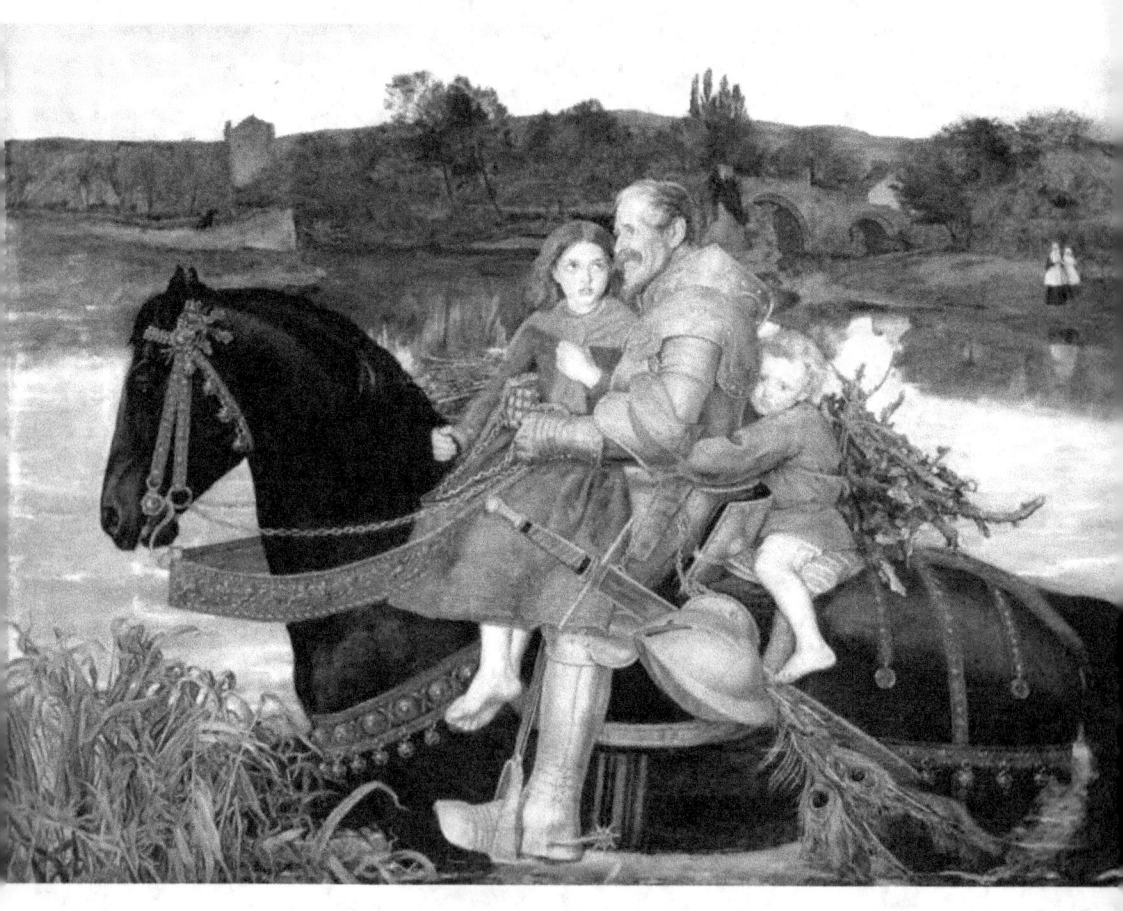

John Everett Millais, Sir Isumbras At the Ford, 1857

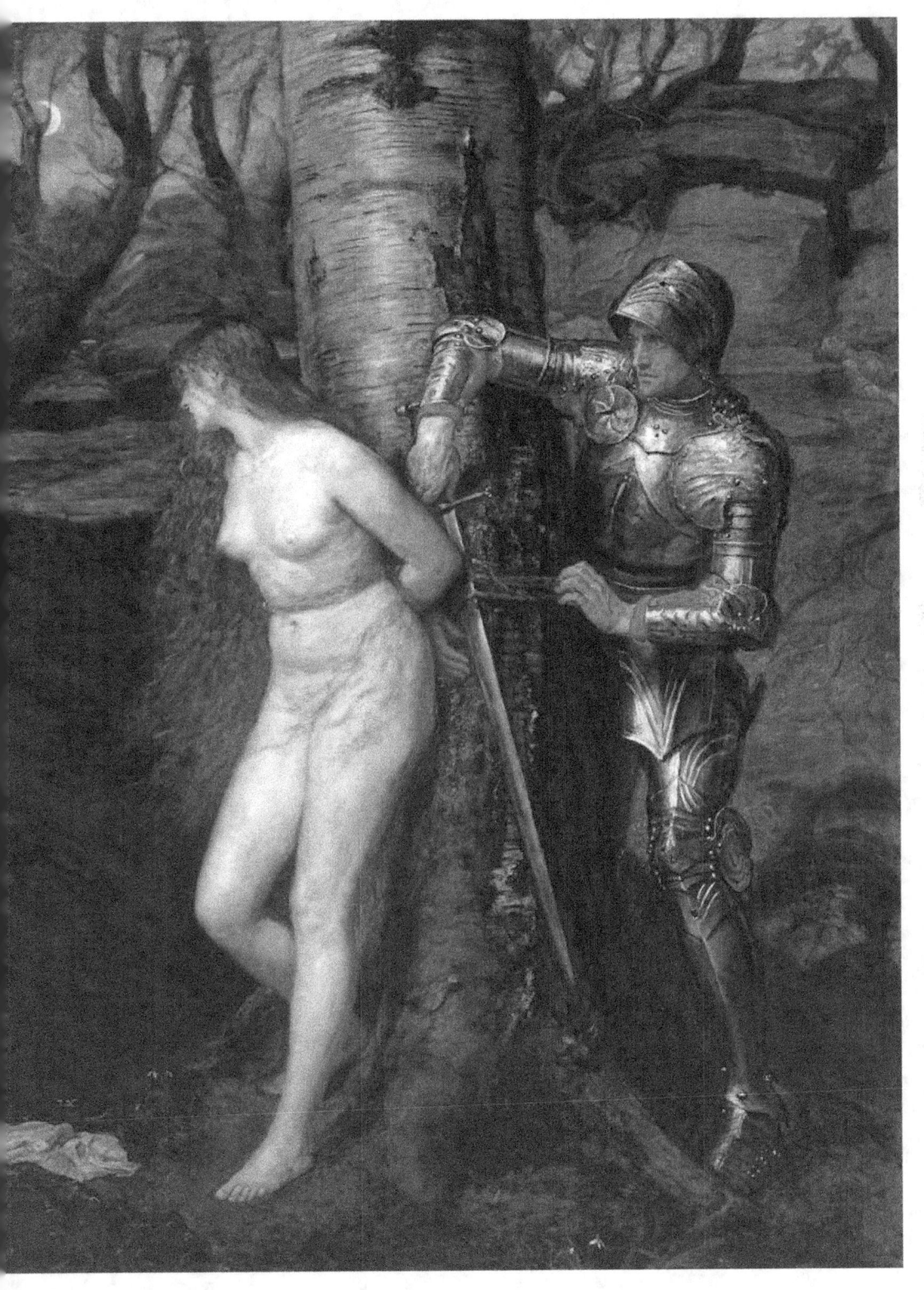

John Everett Millais, The Knight Errant, 1870, Tate, London

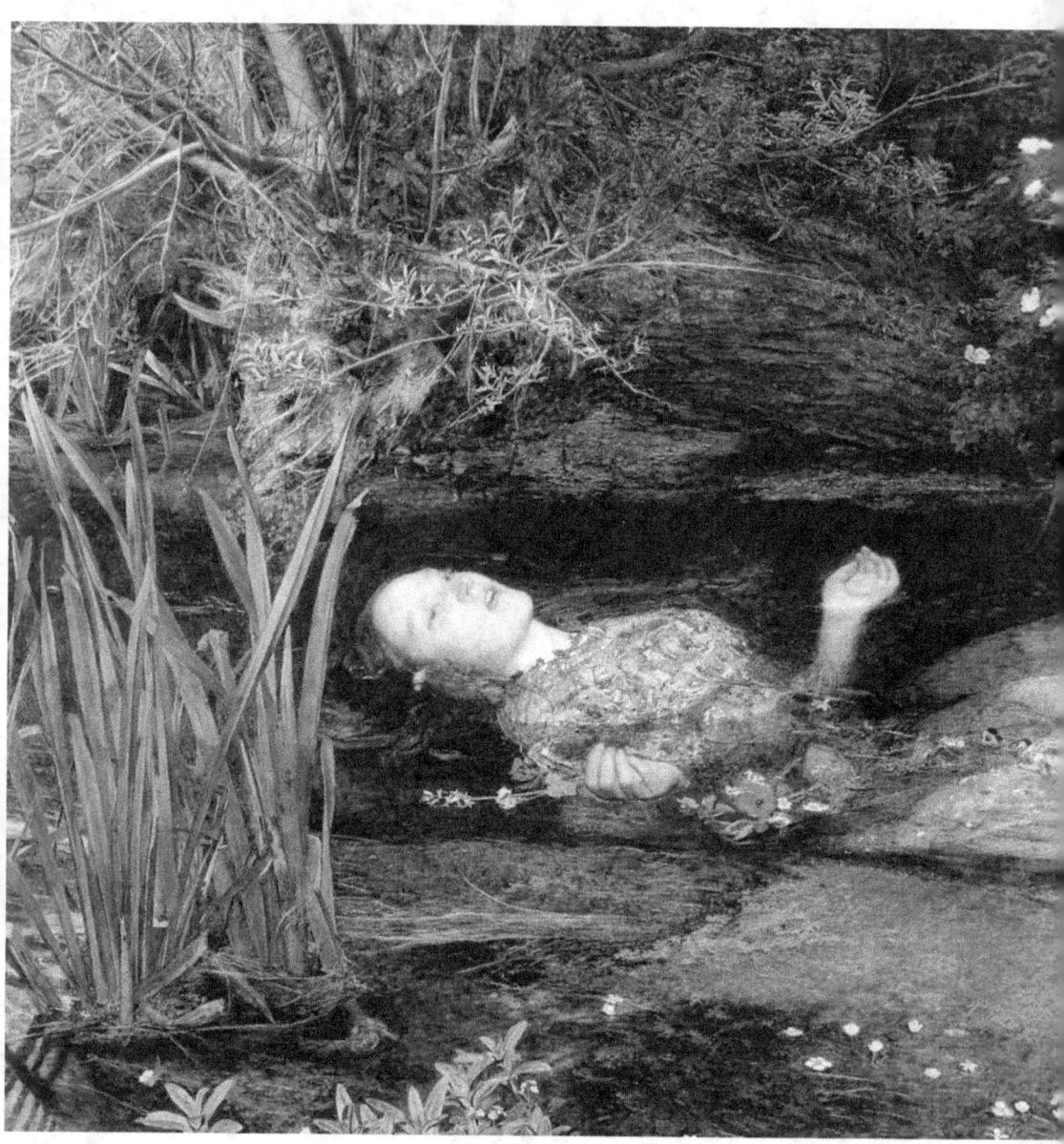

John Everett Millais, Ophelia.

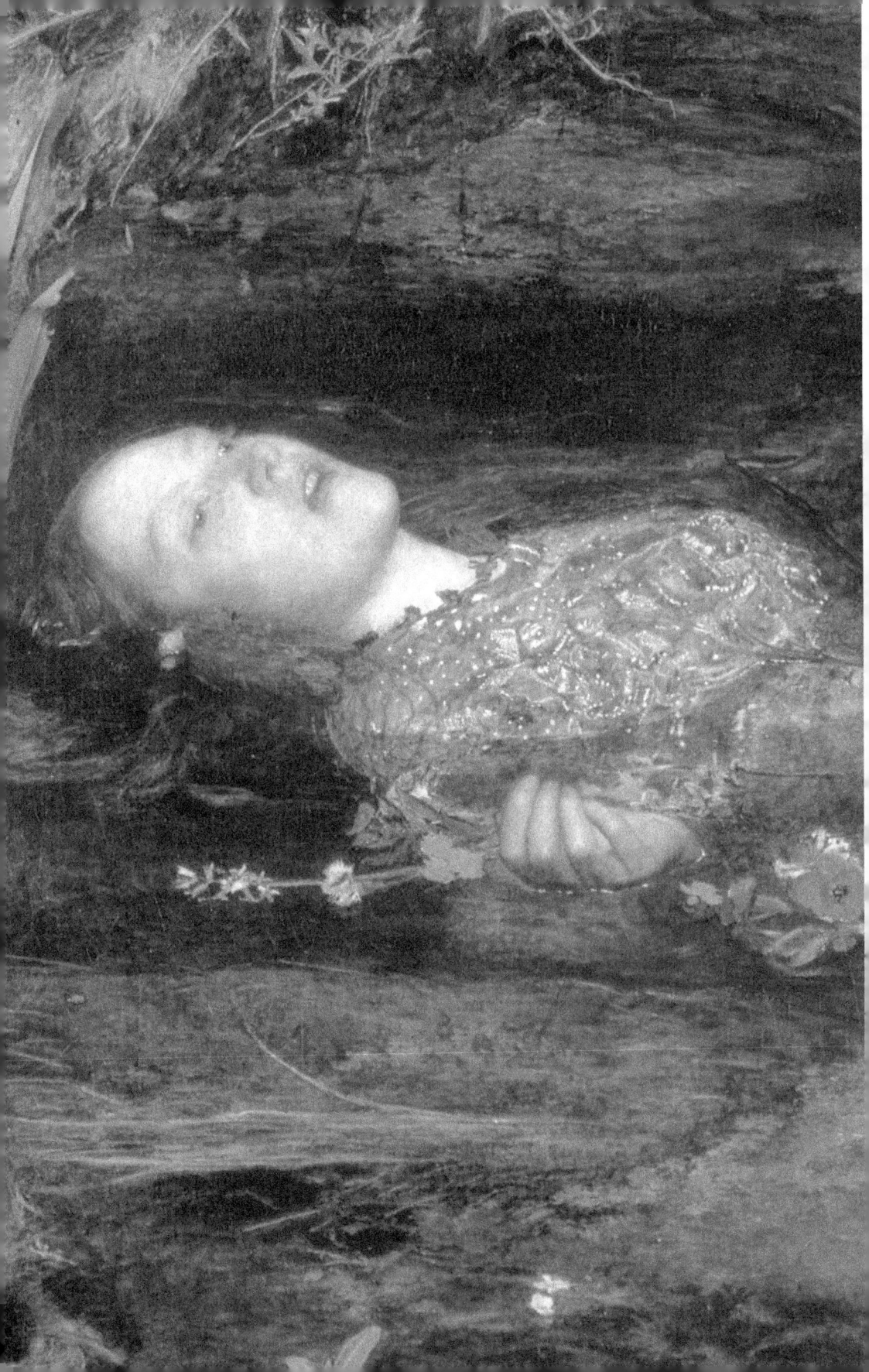

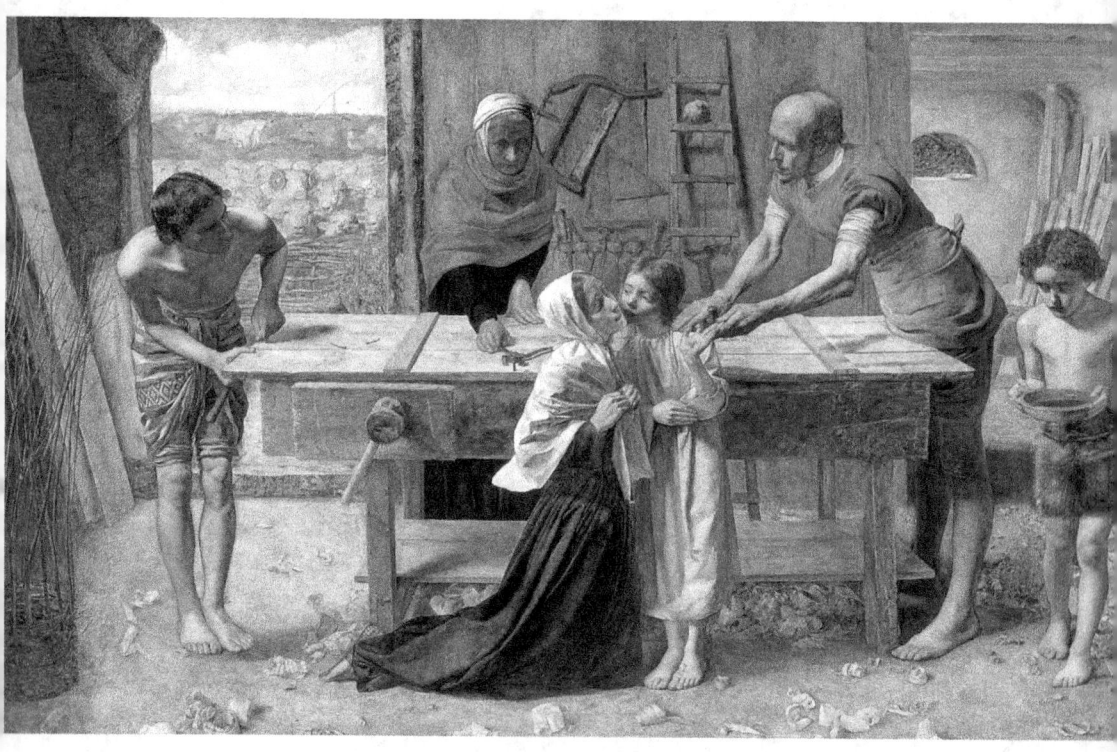

John Everett Millais, Christ In the House of His Parents
(this page and over).

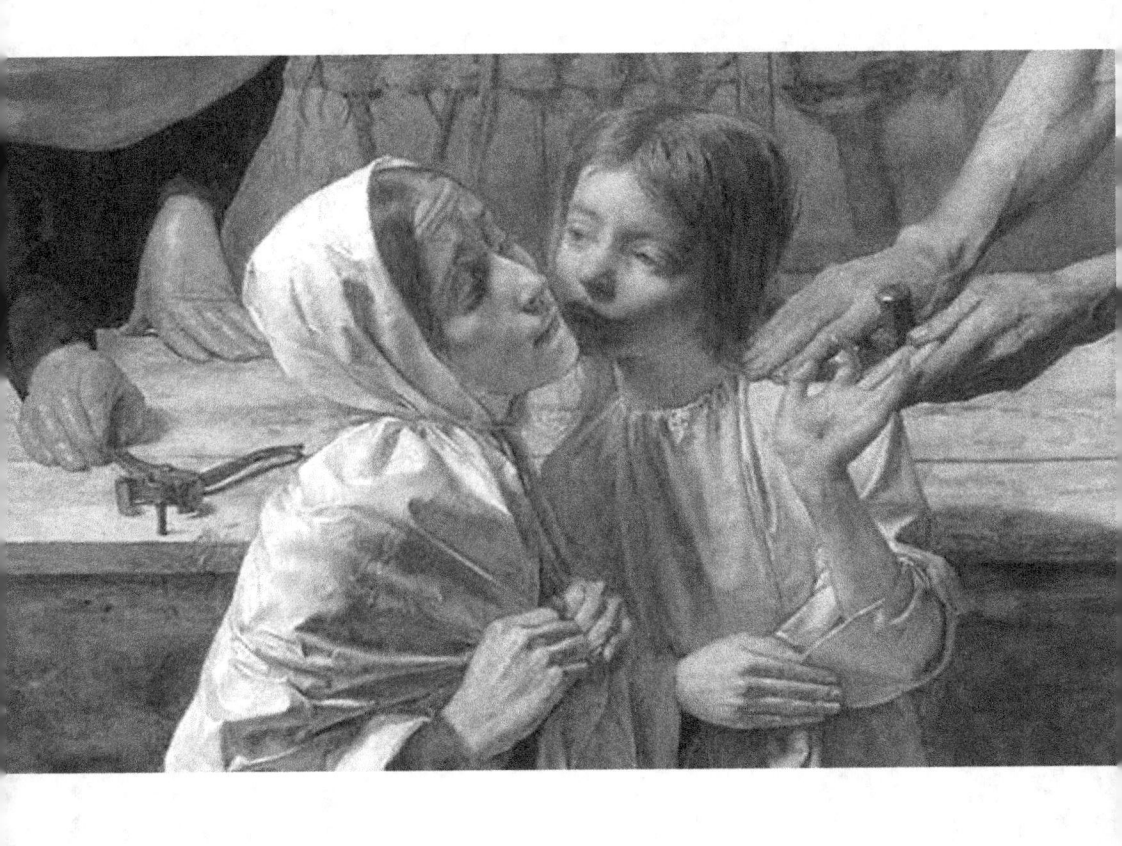

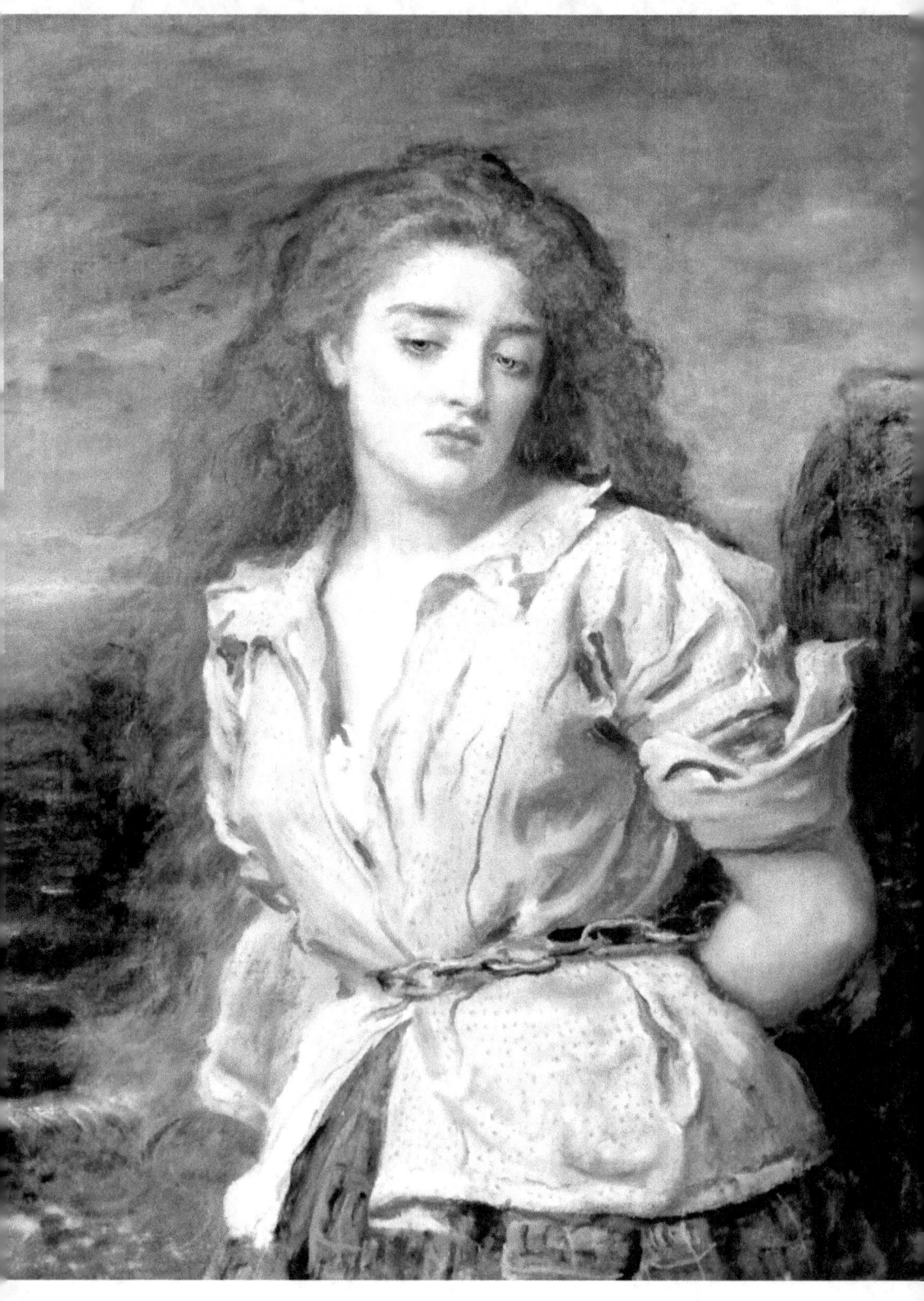

John Everett Millas, The Martyr of the Solway, 1871

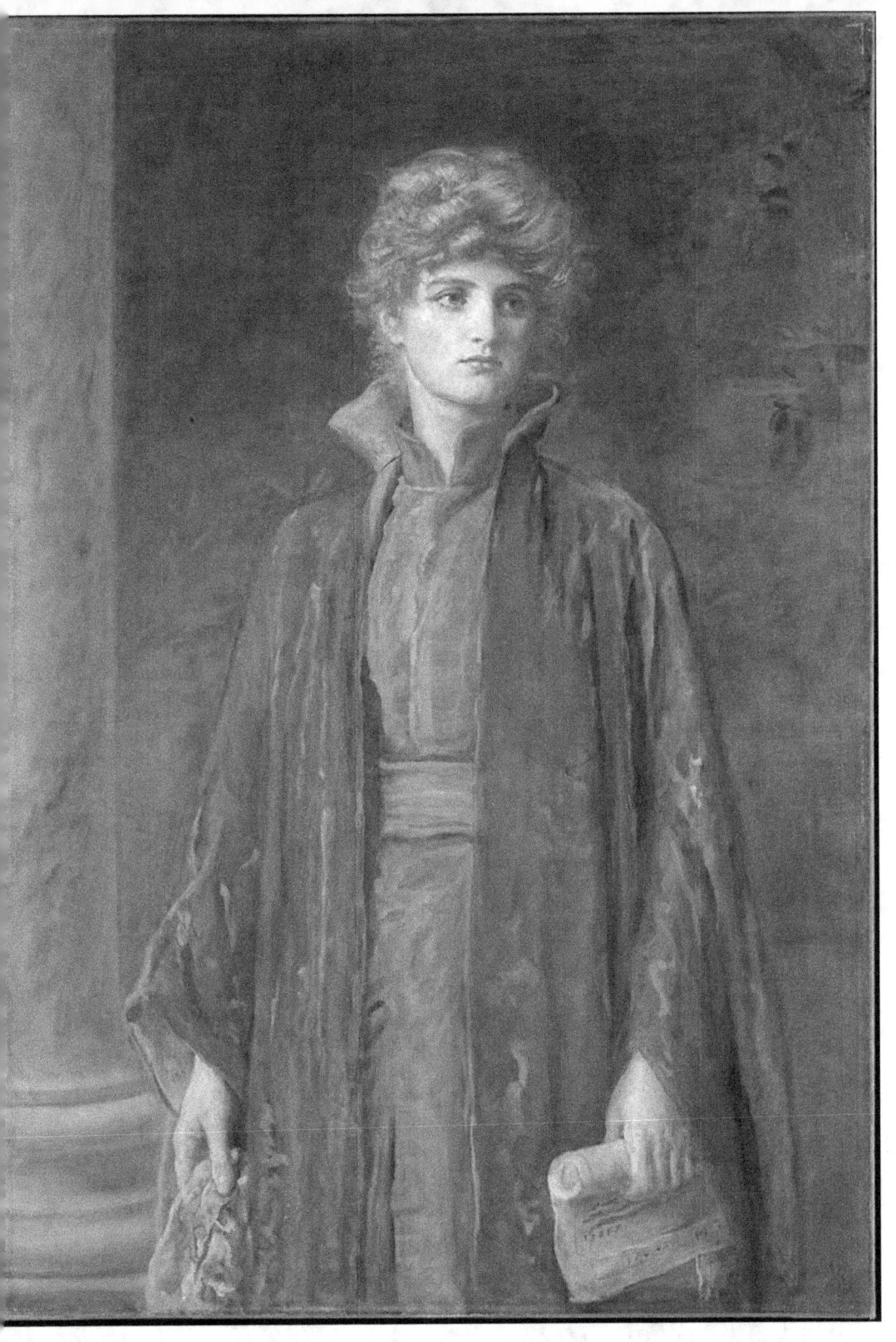

John Everett Millas, Portia, Kate Dolan, 1886, Metropolitan Museum, New York

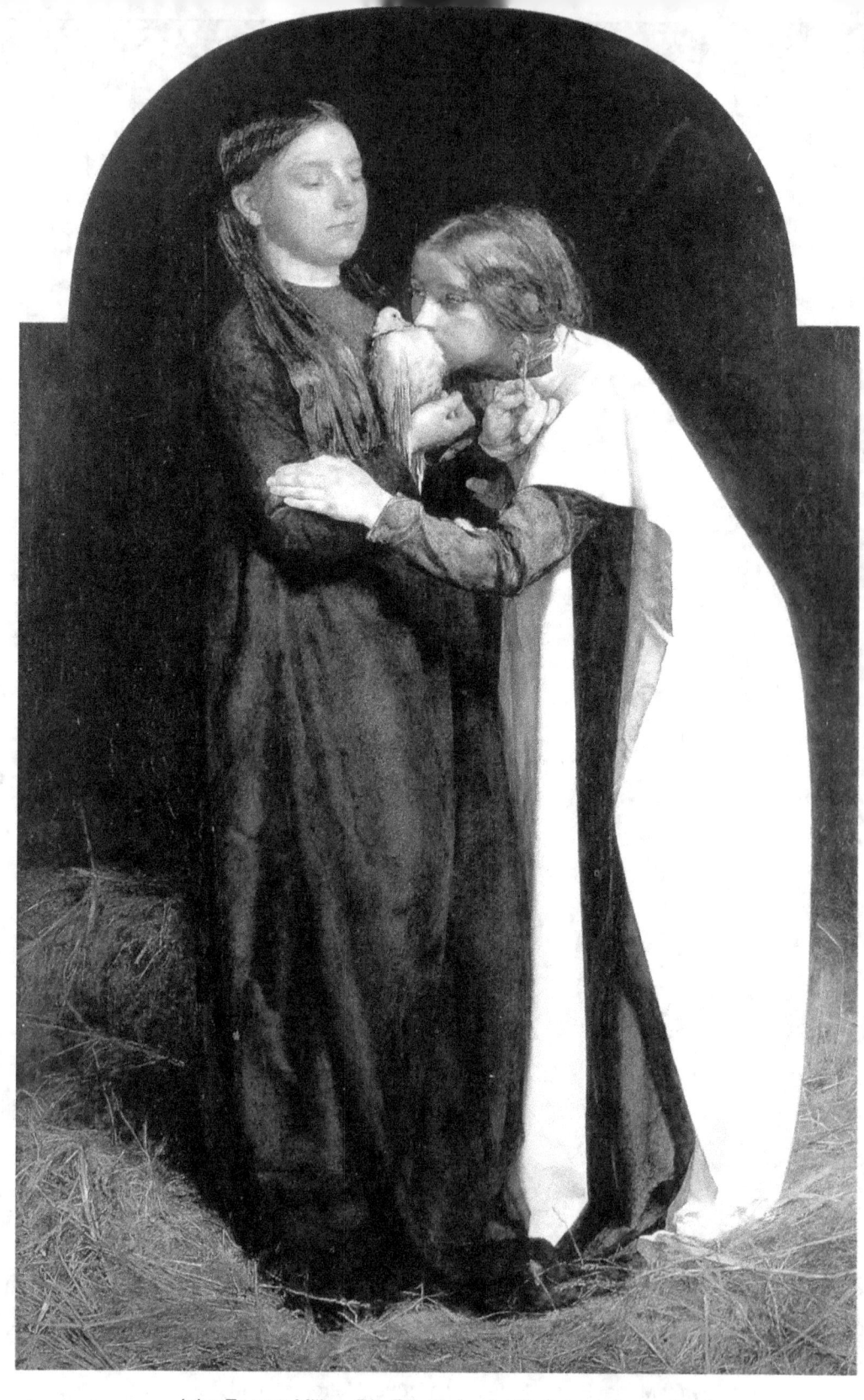

John Everett Millas, Die Rückkehr der Taube zur Arche Noah,
1851, Ashmolean Museum, Oxford

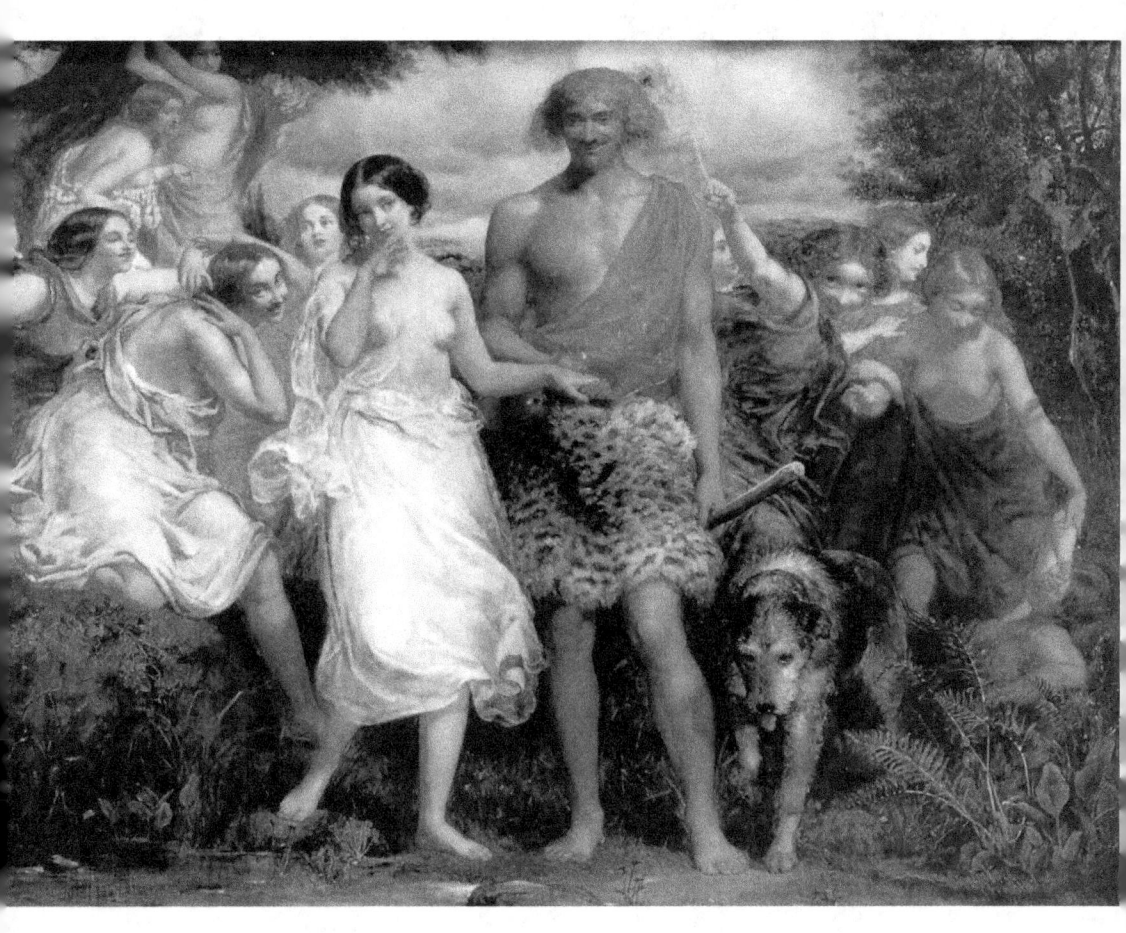

John Everett Millais, Cymon and Iphigenia, 1848, Liverpool.

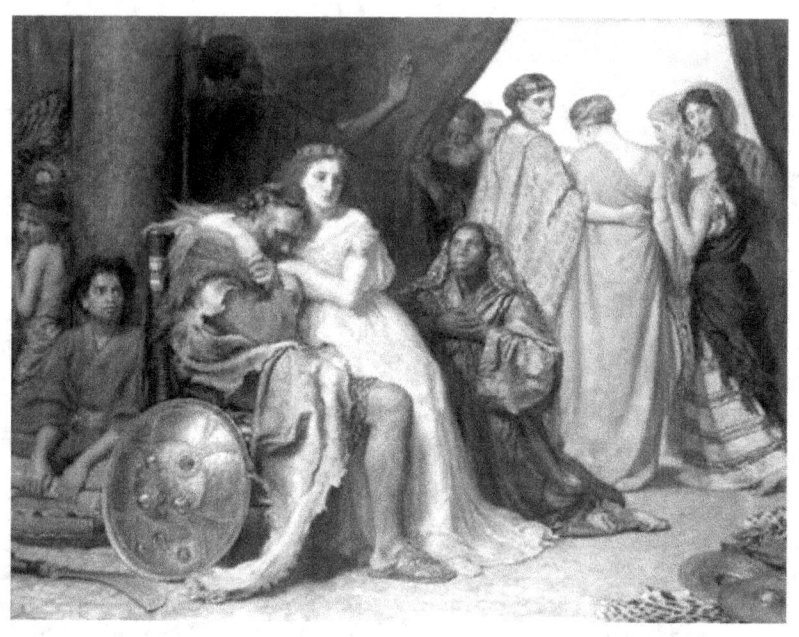

John Everett Millais, Jephthah, 1867

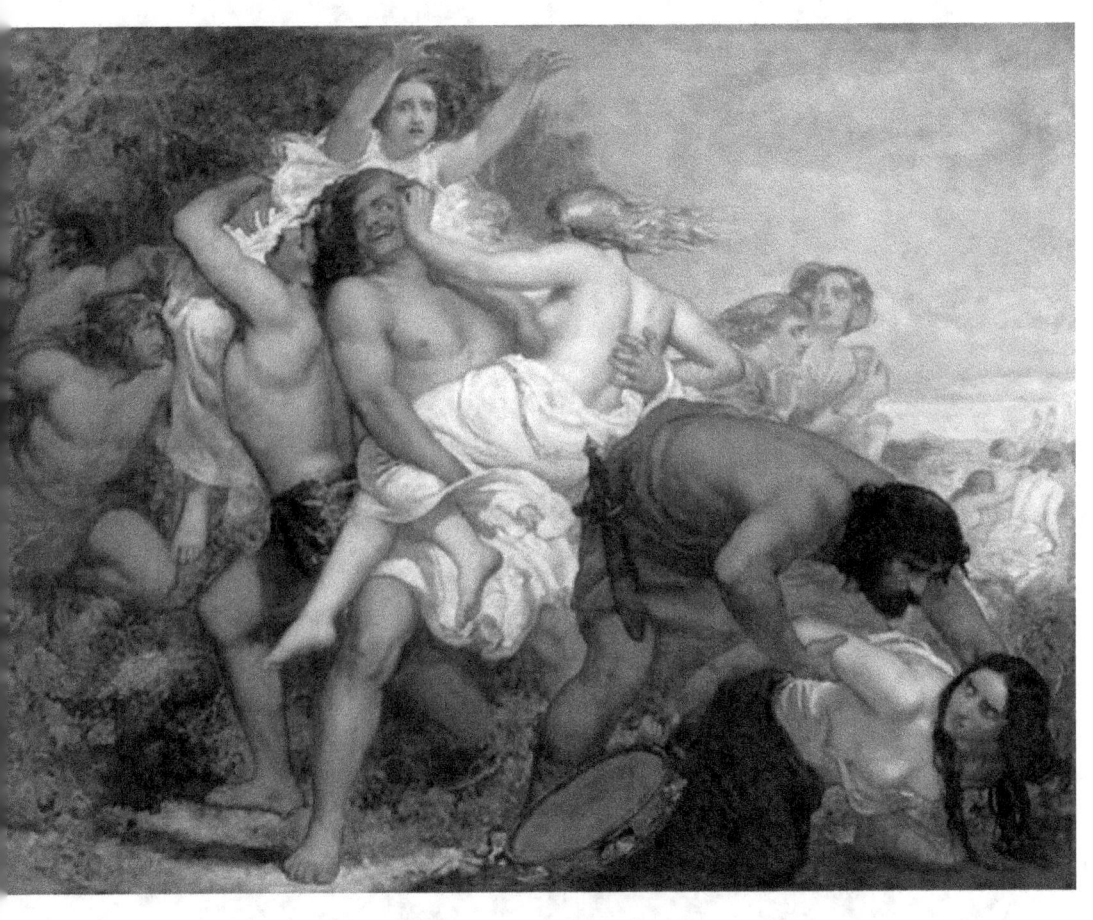

John Everett Millais, Benjamin Seizes the Daughter of Shiloh, 1847

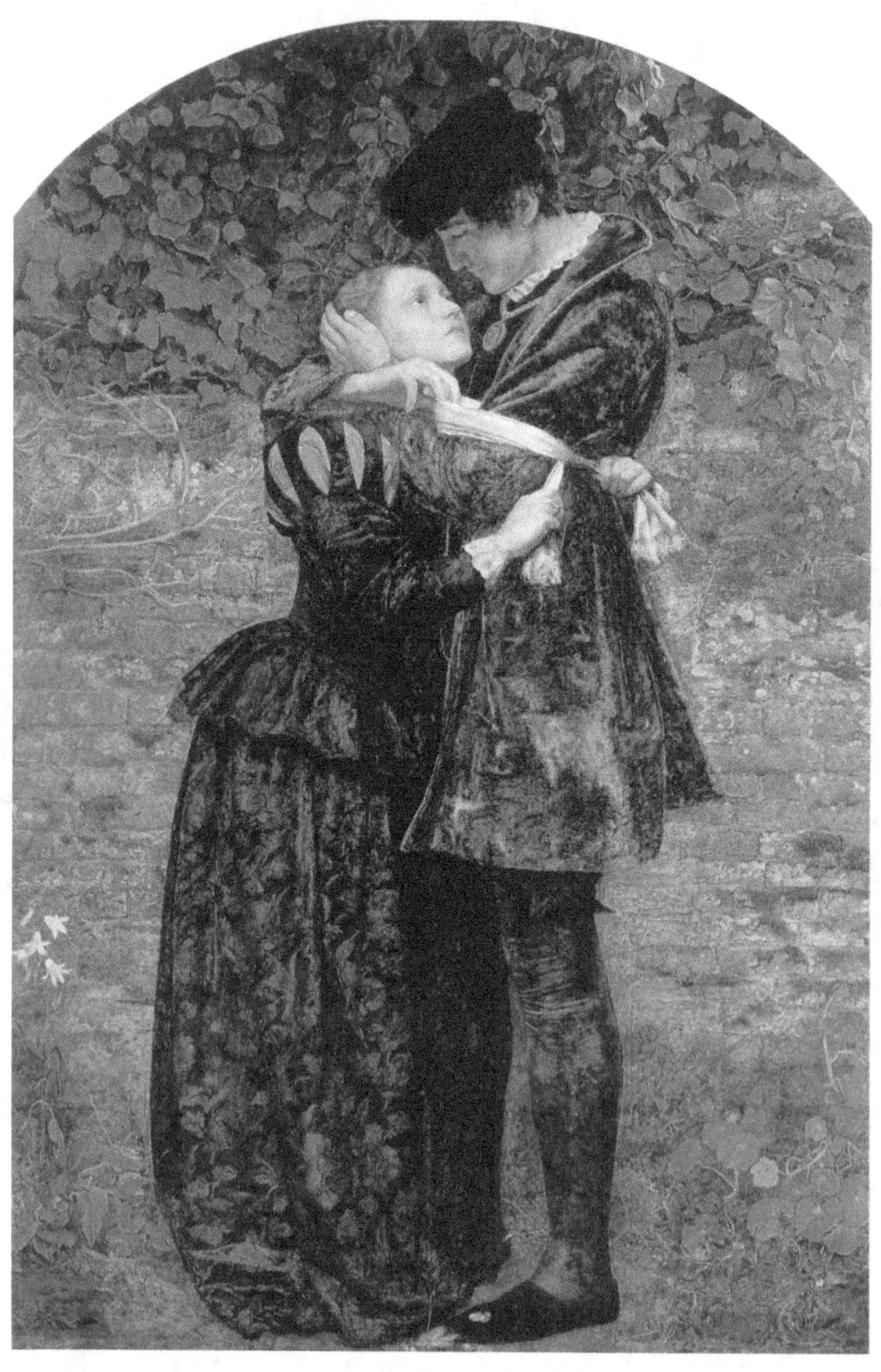

John Everett Millais, A Huguenot, On St Bartholomew's Day, 1851

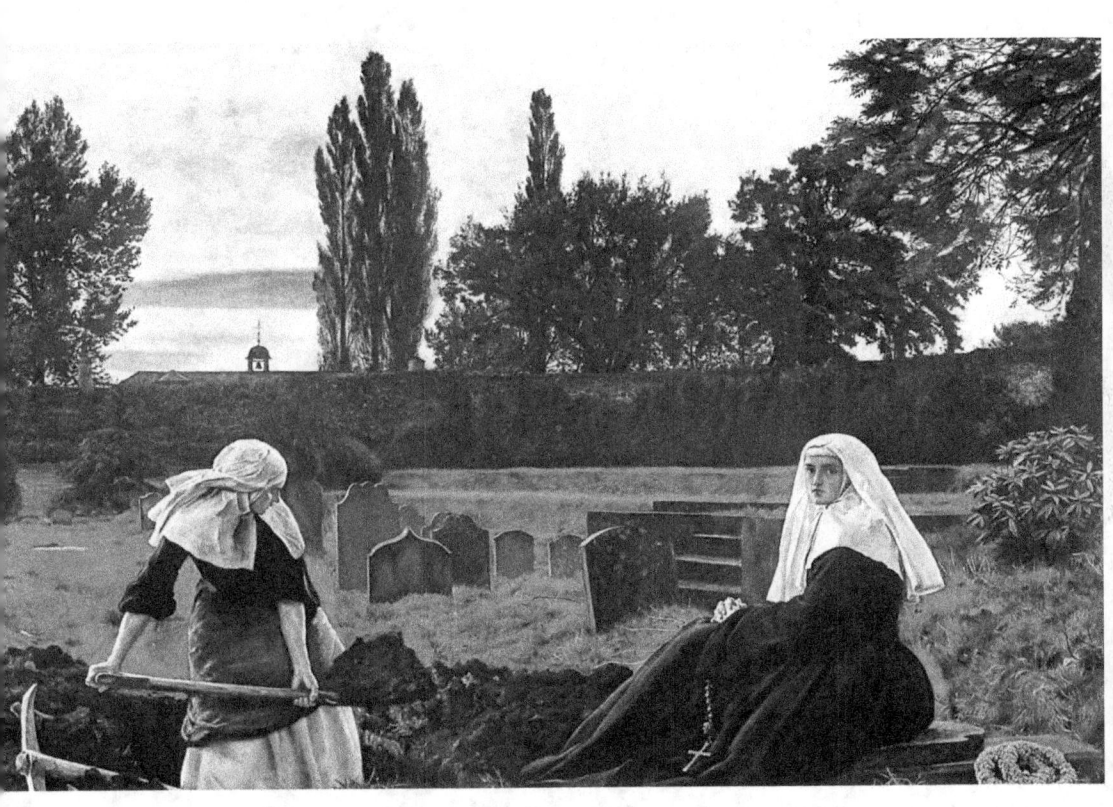

John Everett Millais, The Vale of Rest, 1858, Tate Britain

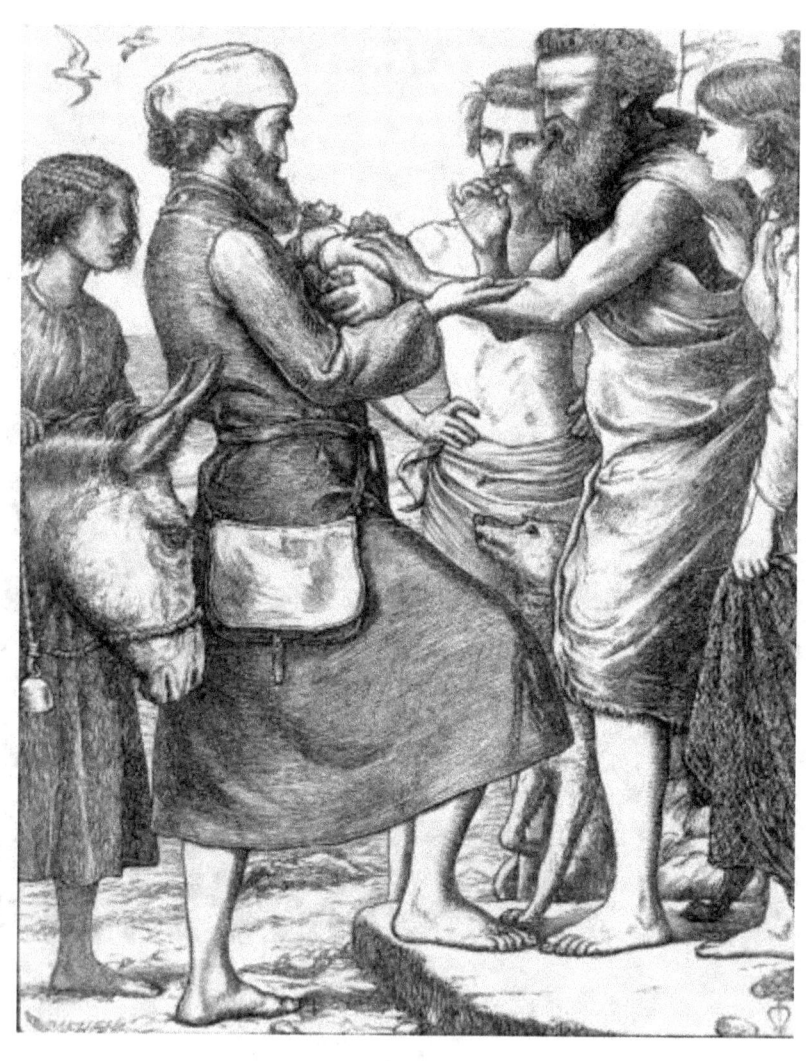

John Everett Millais, Pearl of Great Price, 1864

NOTES ON WORKS

THE ORDER OF RELEASE.
(Tate Gallery)

This is one of the pictures which Millais always reckoned among the greatest of all his successes, and that it has many notable qualities which justify his preference can certainly not be denied. It is wonderful in its earnest and thoughtful realism, and it explains its motive with a completeness that is most convincing. The expression on the face of the woman who brings the order which frees her husband from prison is singularly happy in its combination of tenderness for the wounded Highlander, and triumph over the hesitating gaoler; and there are many other little touches, like the joyous effusiveness of the dog, and the unconsciousness of the sleeping child, which amplify and perfect the pictorial story.

THE BOYHOOD OF RALEIGH
(Tate Gallery)

It would not be inappropriate to describe the "Boyhood of Raleigh" as the prologue to the romance of which the last chapter is written in the "North-West Passage," for in both pictures the artist suggests the fascination of the adventurous life. Young Raleigh and his boy friend are under the spell of the story which the sailor is telling them, a story evidently of engrossing interest and stimulating to the imagination. The faces of the lads show how inspiring they find this tale of strange experiences in lands beyond the sea.

THE KNIGHT ERRANT
(Tate Gallery)

It is generally recognised that the effective representation of the nude figure imposes the severest test not only upon an artist's powers of drawing and painting but upon his sense of æsthetic propriety as well. The "Knight Errant" proves beyond dispute that Millais was able to pass this test triumphantly, for the picture is a magnificent technical achievement and is absolutely discreet in treatment. The subject, a lady rescued from robbers by a wandering knight, is one which occurs frequently in mediæval romance.

AUTUMN LEAVES
(Manchester Art Gallery)

As an example of the quiet and unforced sentiment which characterises so many of the pictures which Millais painted, this delightful composition deserves particular consideration. It has a certain severity of design and solemnity of manner, but in its suggestion of the sadness of autumn there is no trace of morbid sentimentality and no kind of theatrical effect. The picture is a sort of allegory expressed with exquisite tenderness, and with a simple frankness of manner which is especially persuasive.

SPEAK! SPEAK!
(Tate Gallery)

To the man who has loved and lost, the vision of his lady appearing to him as he lies awake at dawn seems so real and living that he begs her to speak to him, and stretches out his arms to clasp what is after all only a creation of his imagination. The dramatic feeling of the picture is as convincing as its pathos; the painter has grasped completely the possibilities of his subject, and he tells his story with just the touch of mystery needed to give it due significance. The management of the light and shade, and of the contrast between the warm lamplight and the greyness of the early morning, is full of both power and subtlety.

THE VALE OF REST
(Tate Gallery)

None of the pictures which can be assigned to the period when Millais was still a strict adherent to the Pre-Raphaelite creed can be said to surpass "The Vale of Rest" in depth and purity of feeling; and certainly none expresses better in its character and manner of treatment the artist's conception. The same exquisite sentiment, sincere and dignified, which distinguishes "Autumn Leaves" gives to "The Vale of Rest" an absorbing interest; and the way in which every detail of the composition and every subtlety in the arrangement and expression of the subject have been used to enhance the effect which the artist intended to produce, claims unqualified admiration.

OPHELIA
(Tate Gallery)

Realism more searching and more significant than that which Millais sought for and attained in this small canvas would hardly come within the bounds of possibility. But the picture is much more than a simple study of facts; it has an exquisite charm of poetic feeling, and it is conceived with a full measure of the tenderness needed in a representation of the most pathetic of all Shakespeare's heroines. Such a work has a place, definite and indisputable, among the classics of art, and counts as one of the chief masterpieces of the British School.

THE NORTH-WEST PASSAGE
(Tate Gallery)

Even if the "North-West Passage" were not the masterly piece of painting that it is, it would still be a picture of importance because it appeals so vividly to the national spirit of adventure. The old Arctic explorer, no longer able to satisfy his still strenuous inclinations, listens to the record of his past activities which is being read to him by his daughter, and yearns once more to battle with the hardships which must be faced by the traveller in the frozen north. The old man's head, one of the finest technical achievements in modern art, was painted from Trelawny, the friend of Byron, and Shelley.

On the following pages are illustrations of some of the contemporaries of Millais.

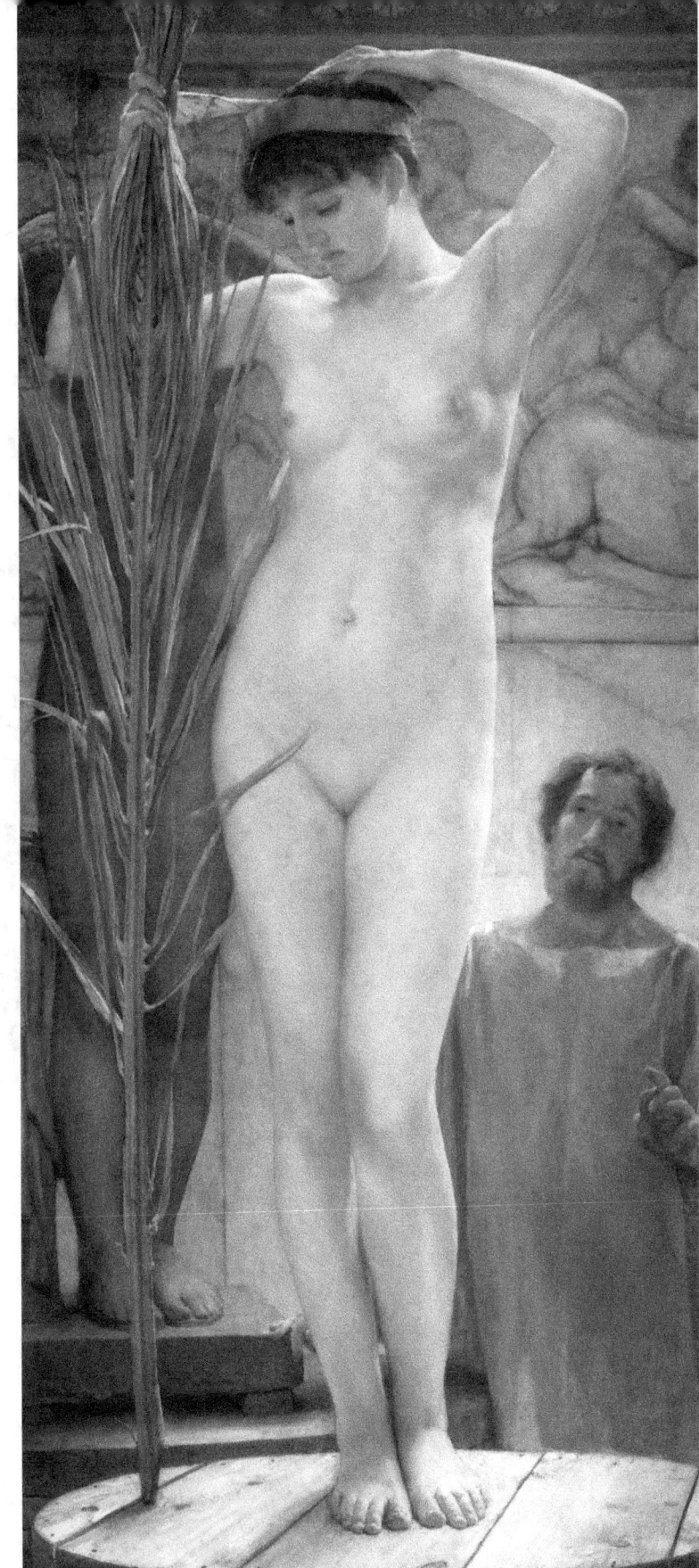

Lawrence
Alma-Tadema,
A Sculptor's Model,
1877, private
collection

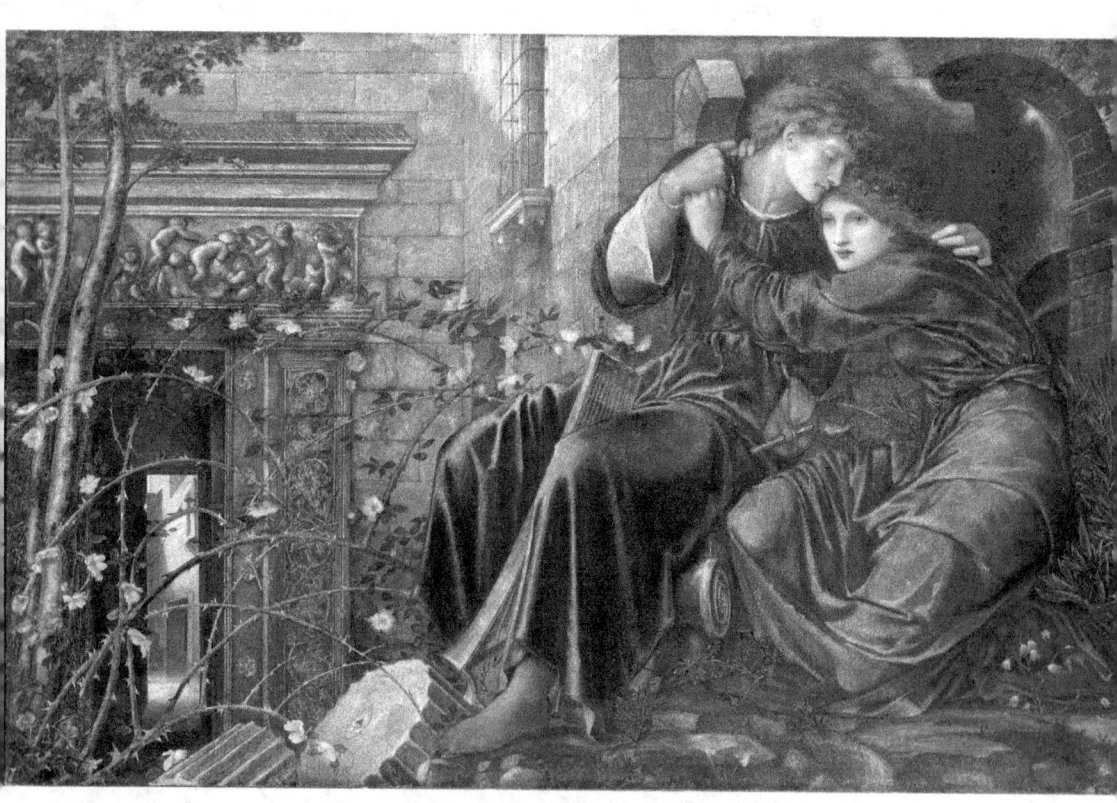

Edward Burne-Jones, Love Among the Ruins, 1873

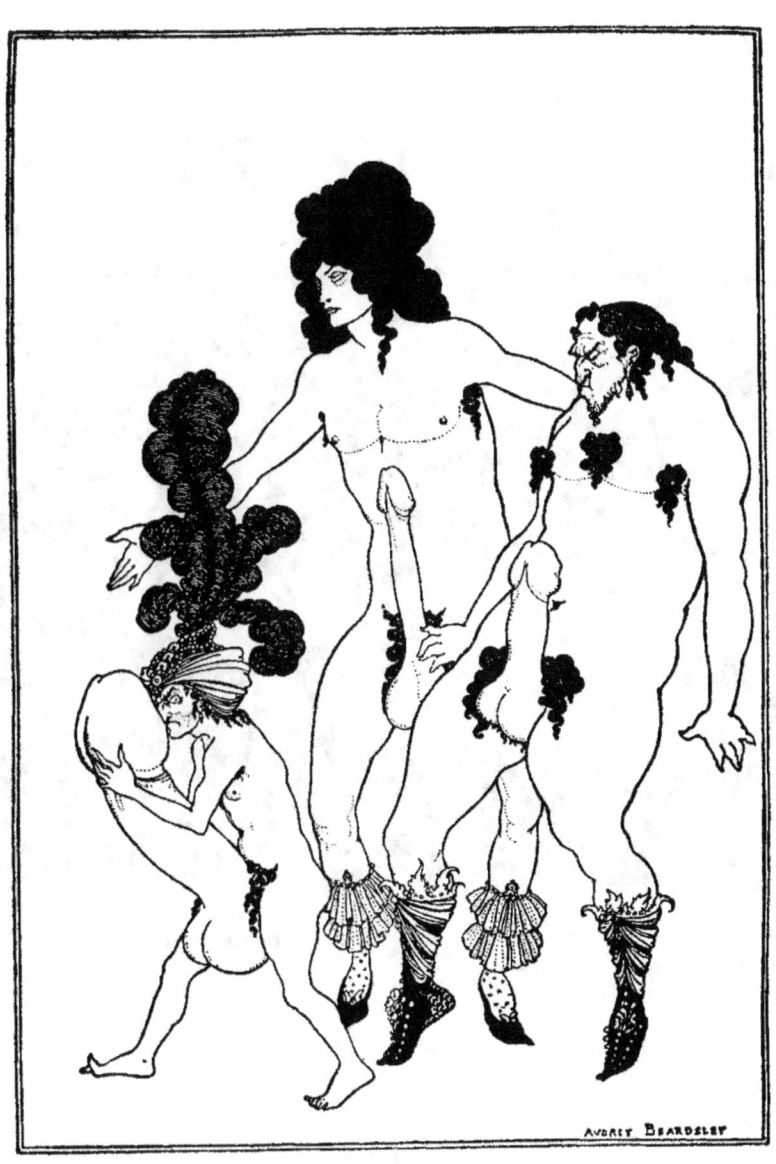

Aubrey Beardsley, Aristophanes, Lysistrata, 1896

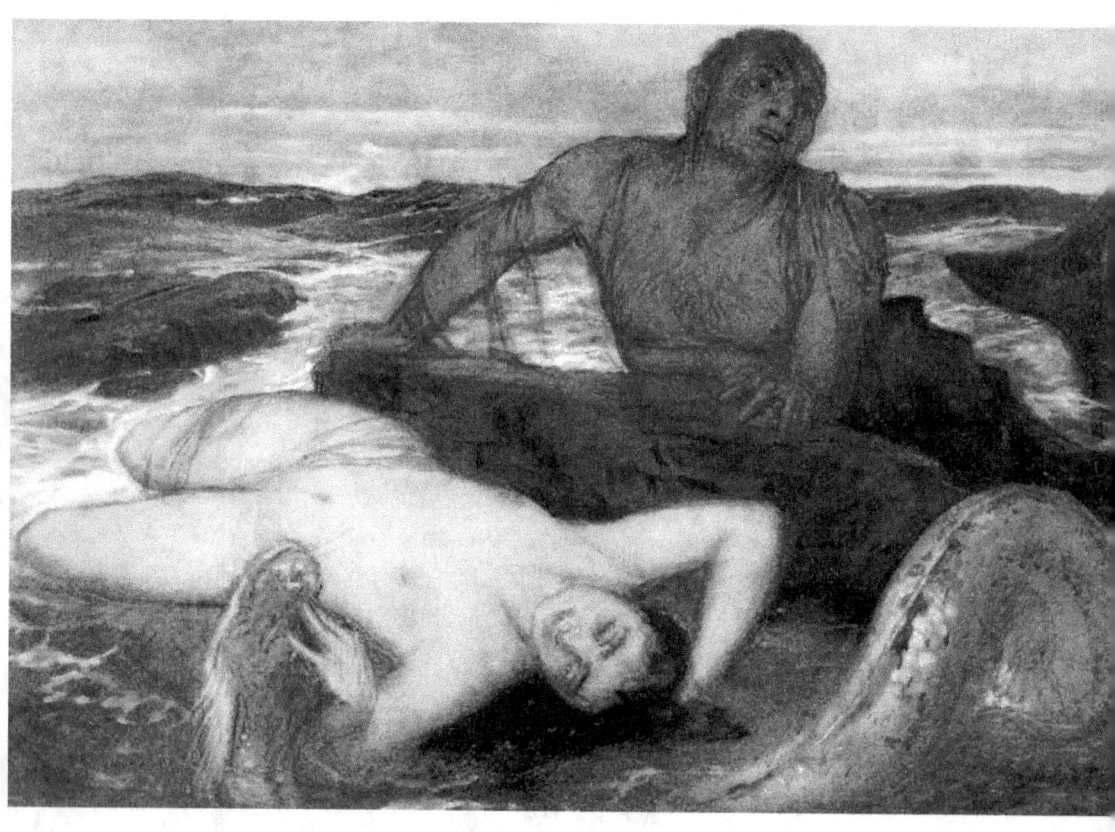

Arnold Böcklin, Triton and Nereid, 1877

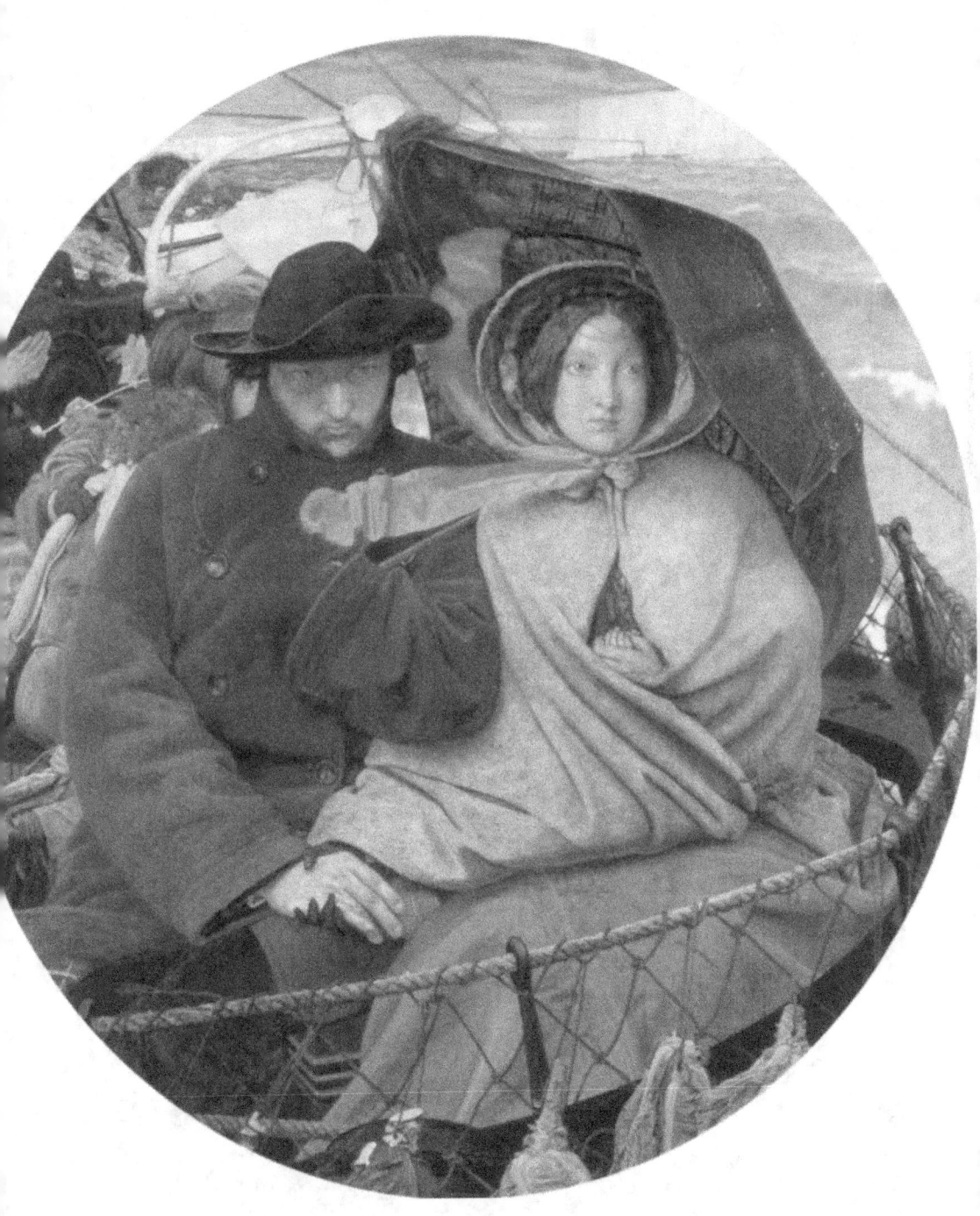

Ford Madox Brown, The Last of England, 1855,
Birmingham

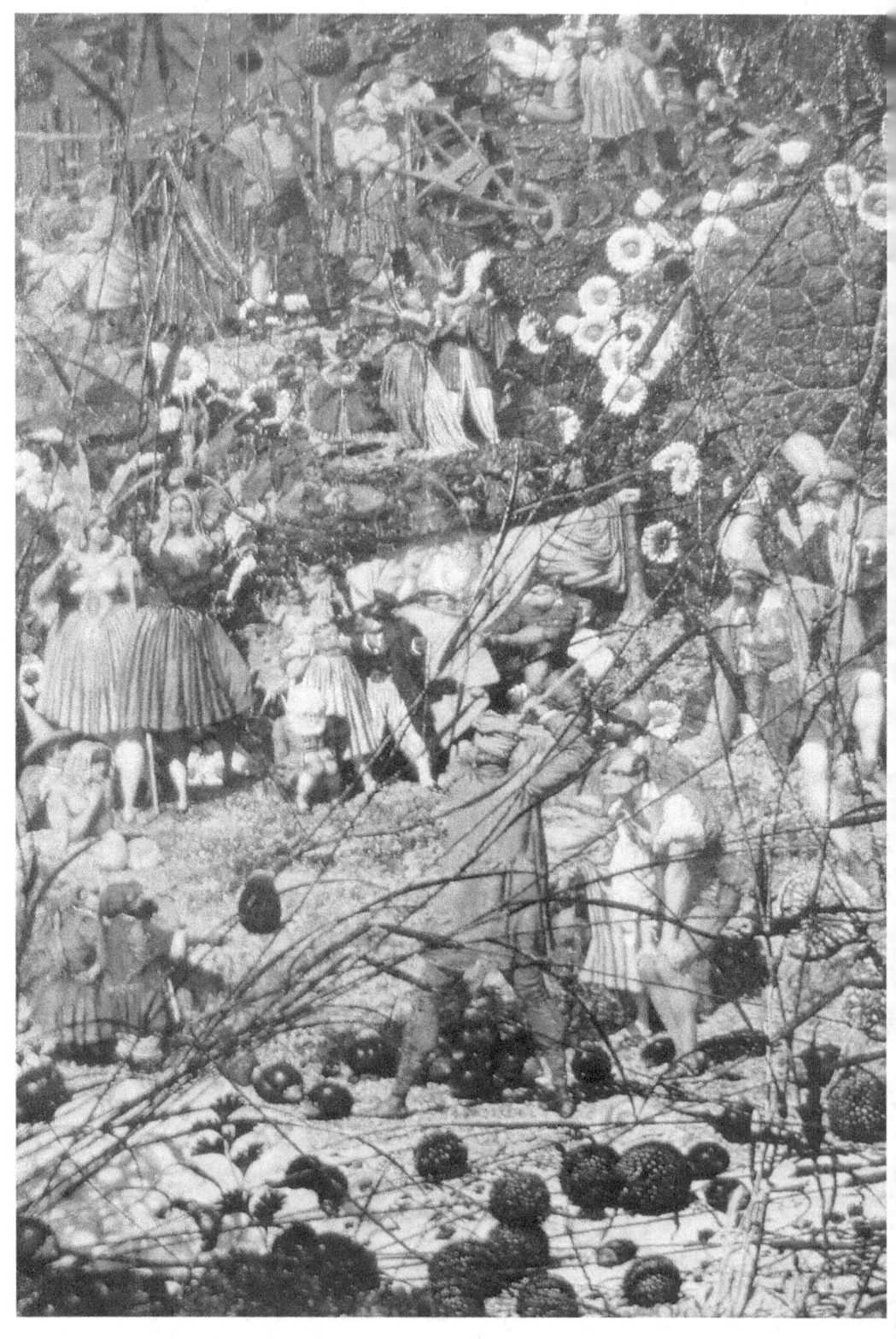

Richard Dadd, The Fairy-Feller's Master-Stroke, Tate, London

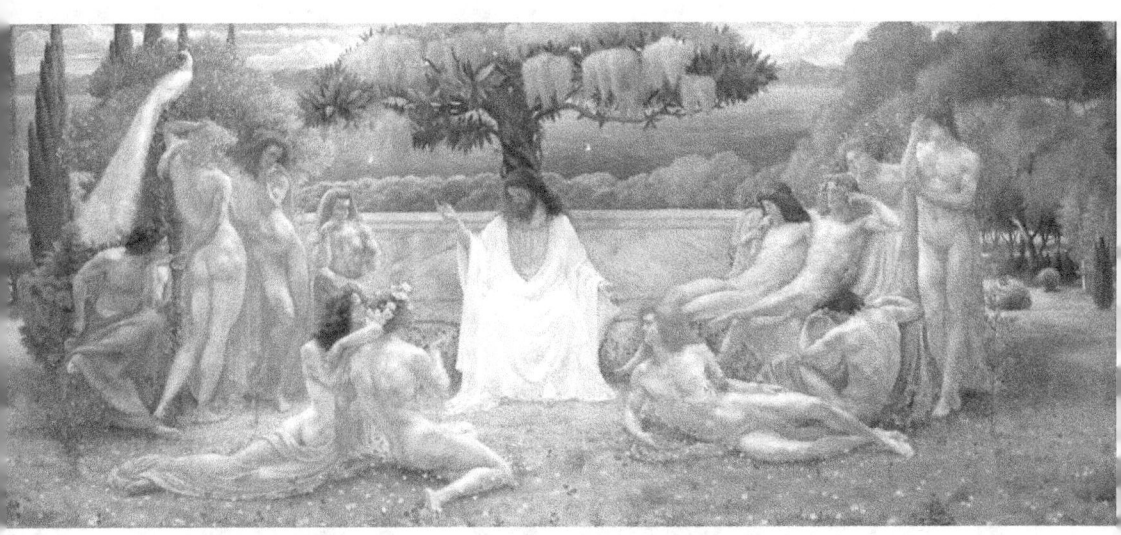

Jean Delville, The School of Plato, 1898

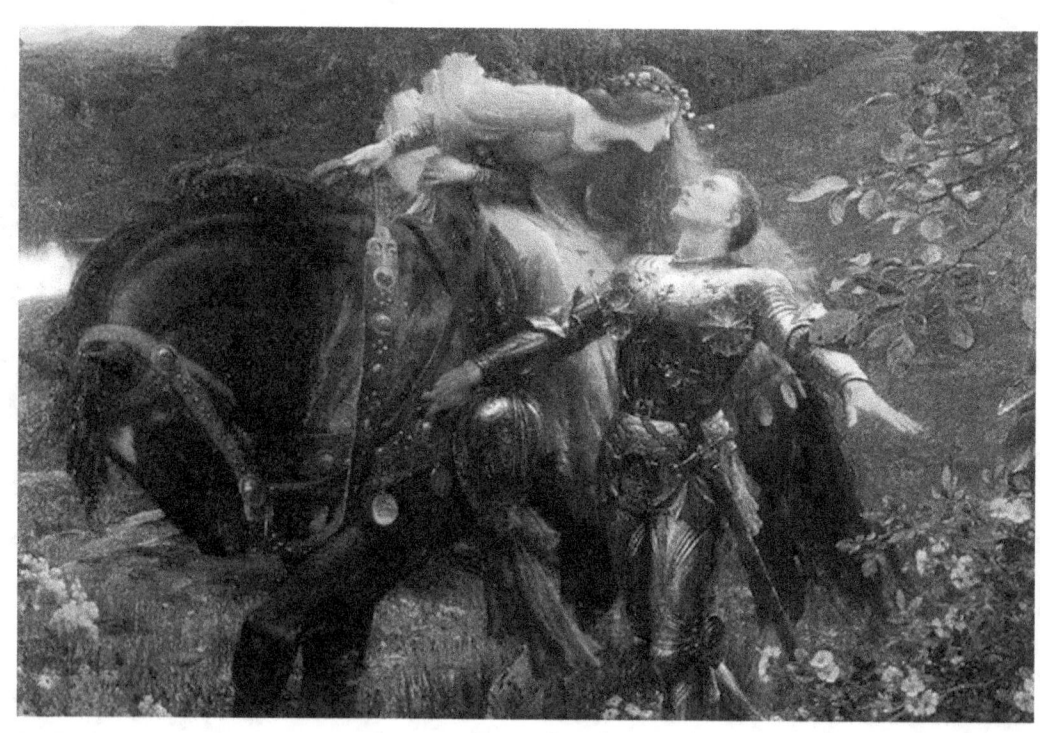

Sir Francis Dicksee, 'La Belle Dame Sans Merci'

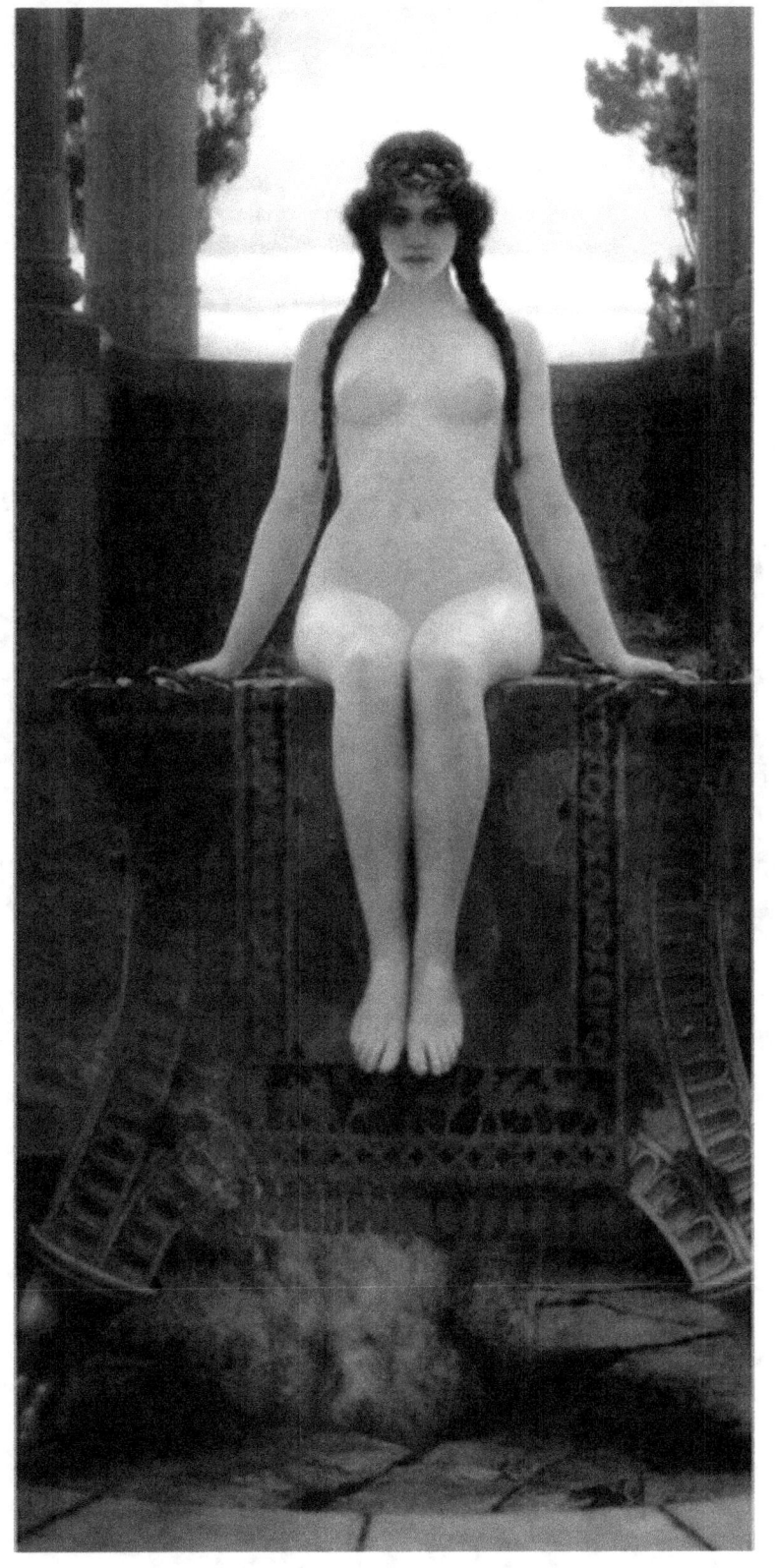

John Godward, The Delphic Oracle, 1899

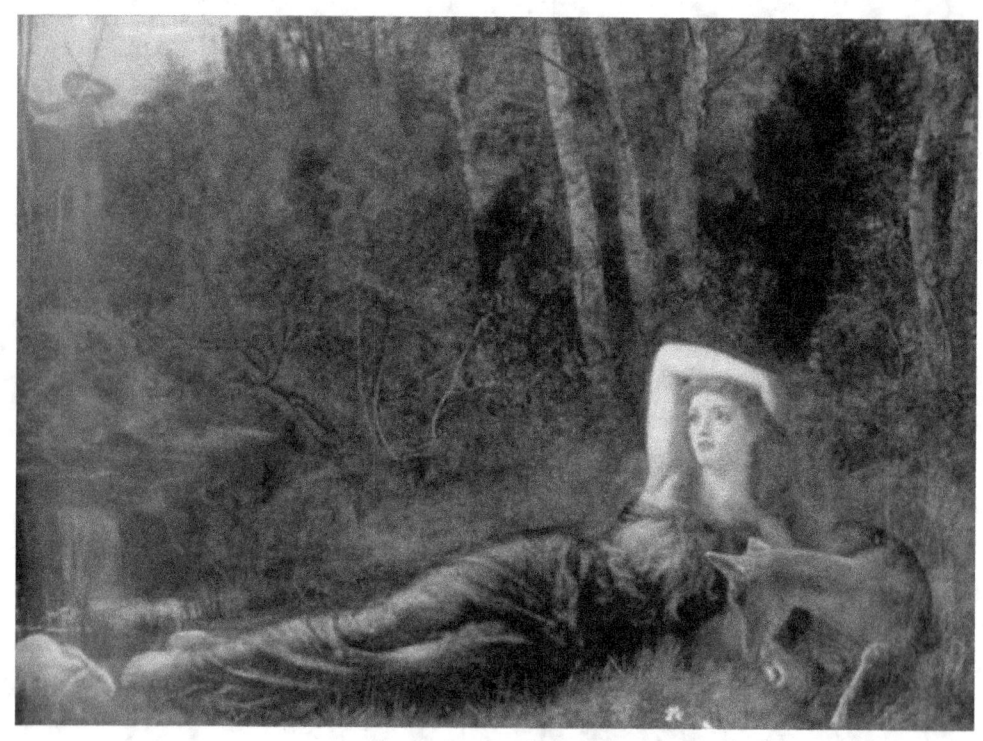

Arthur Hughes, Endymion

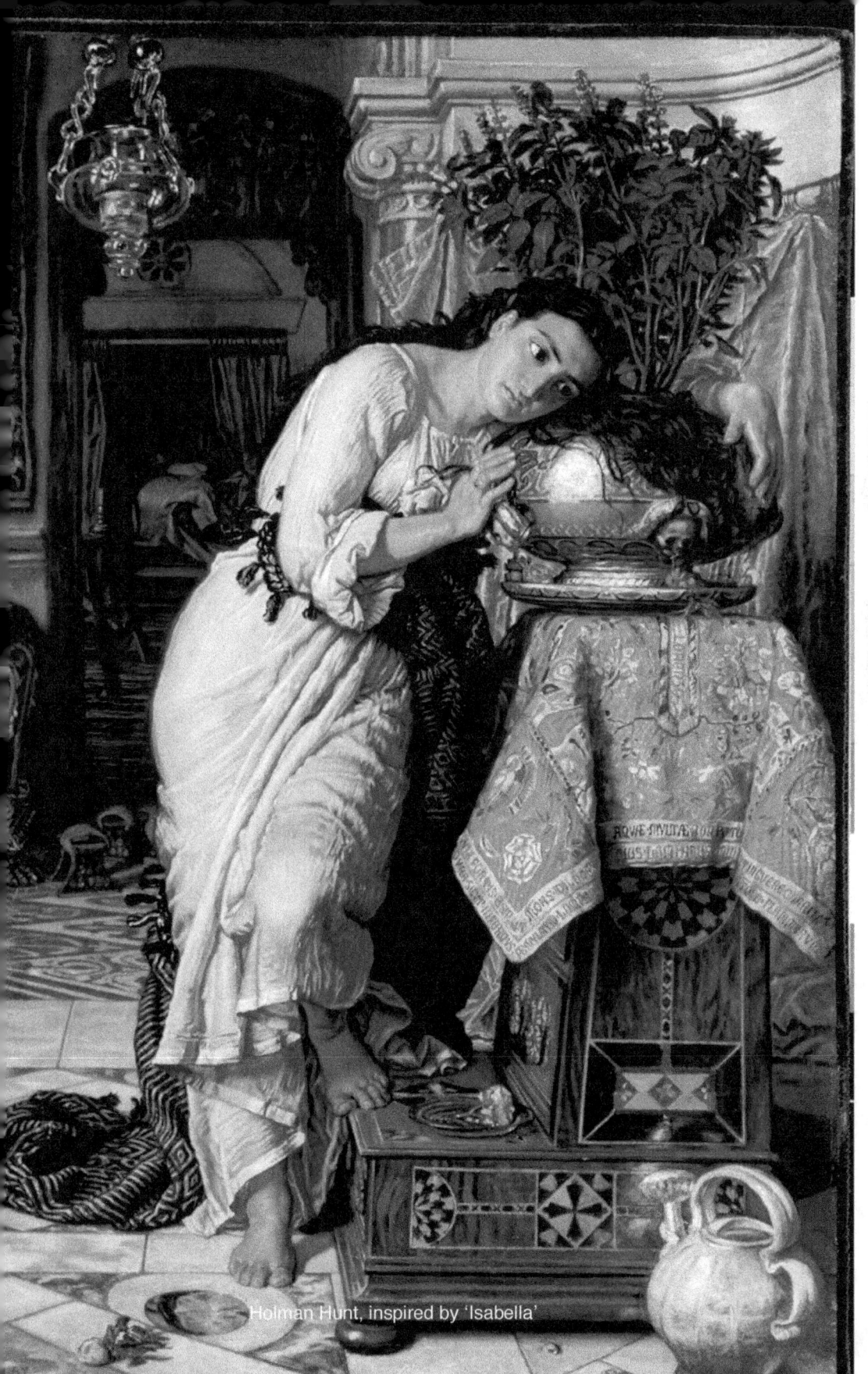

Holman Hunt, inspired by 'Isabella'

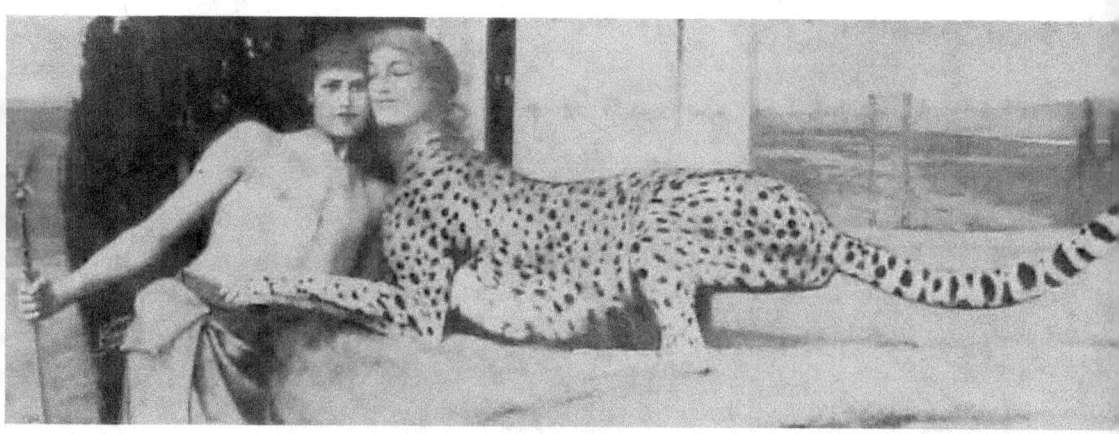

Fernand Knopff, The Caresses of the Sphinx, 1896, Brussels

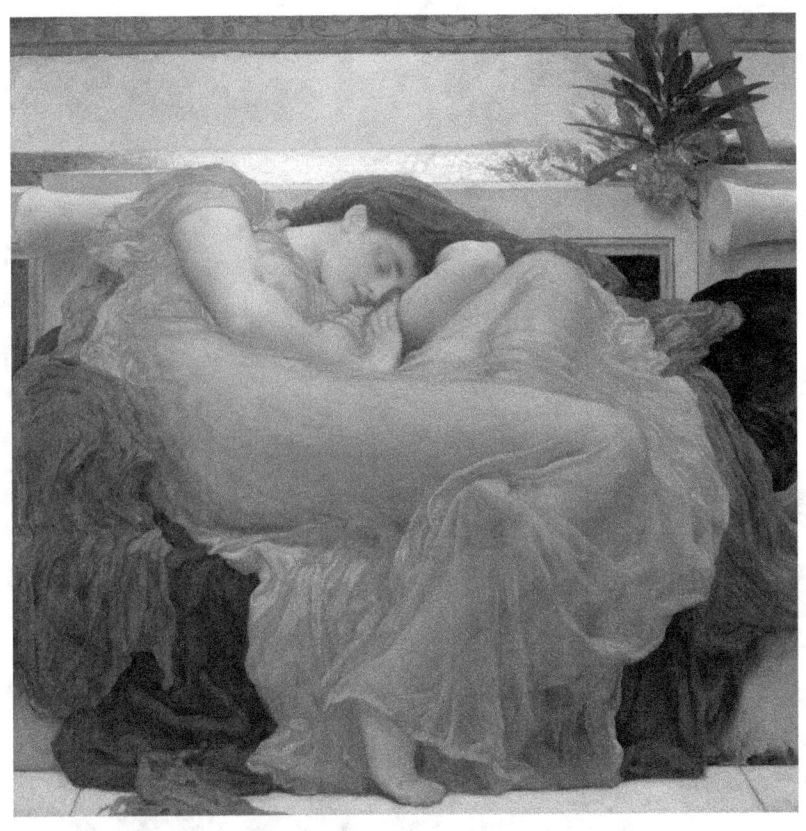

Lord Leighton, Flaming June, 1895, Puerto Rico

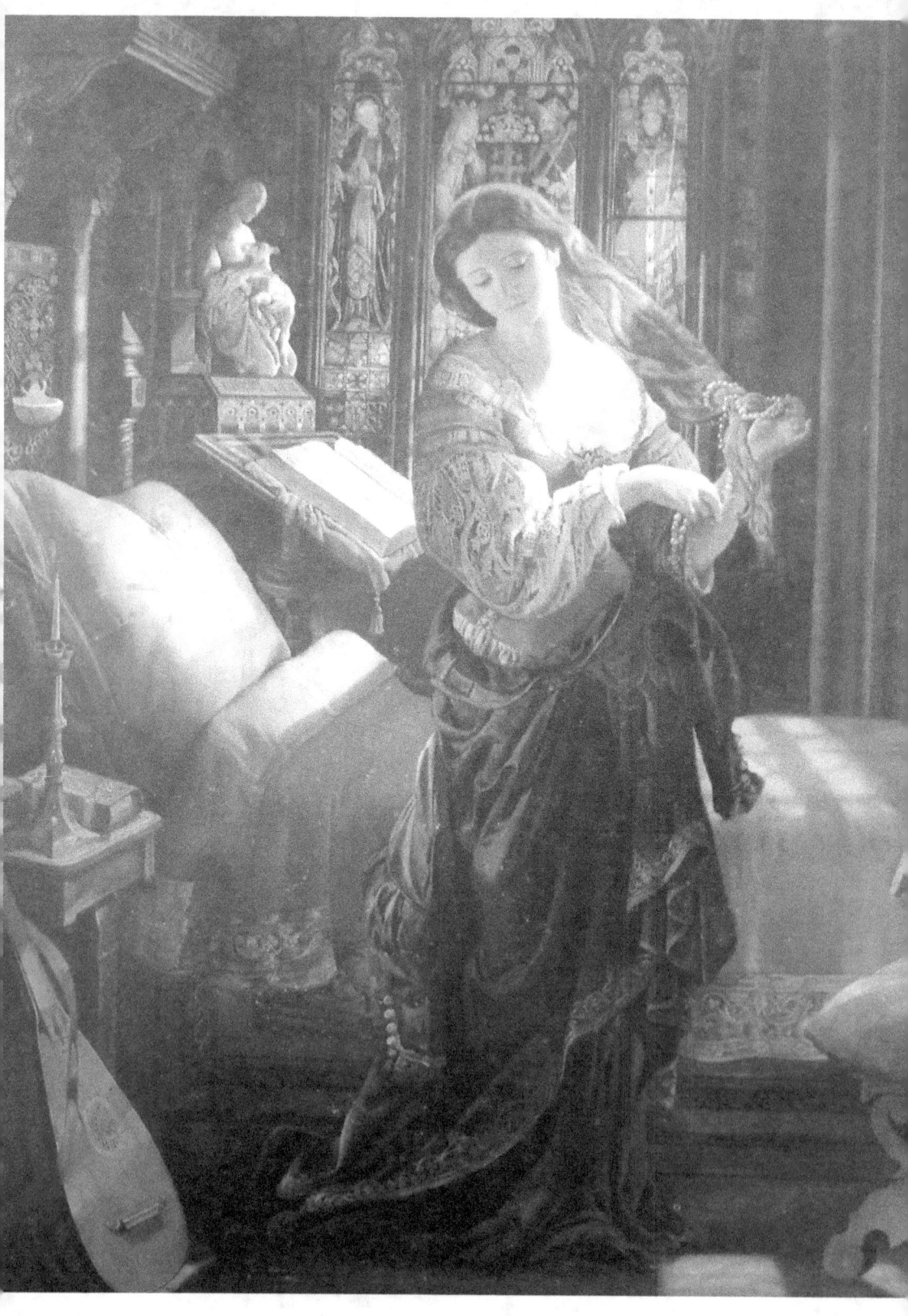

Daniel Maclise, Madeline After Prayer, 1868, Walker Art Gallery

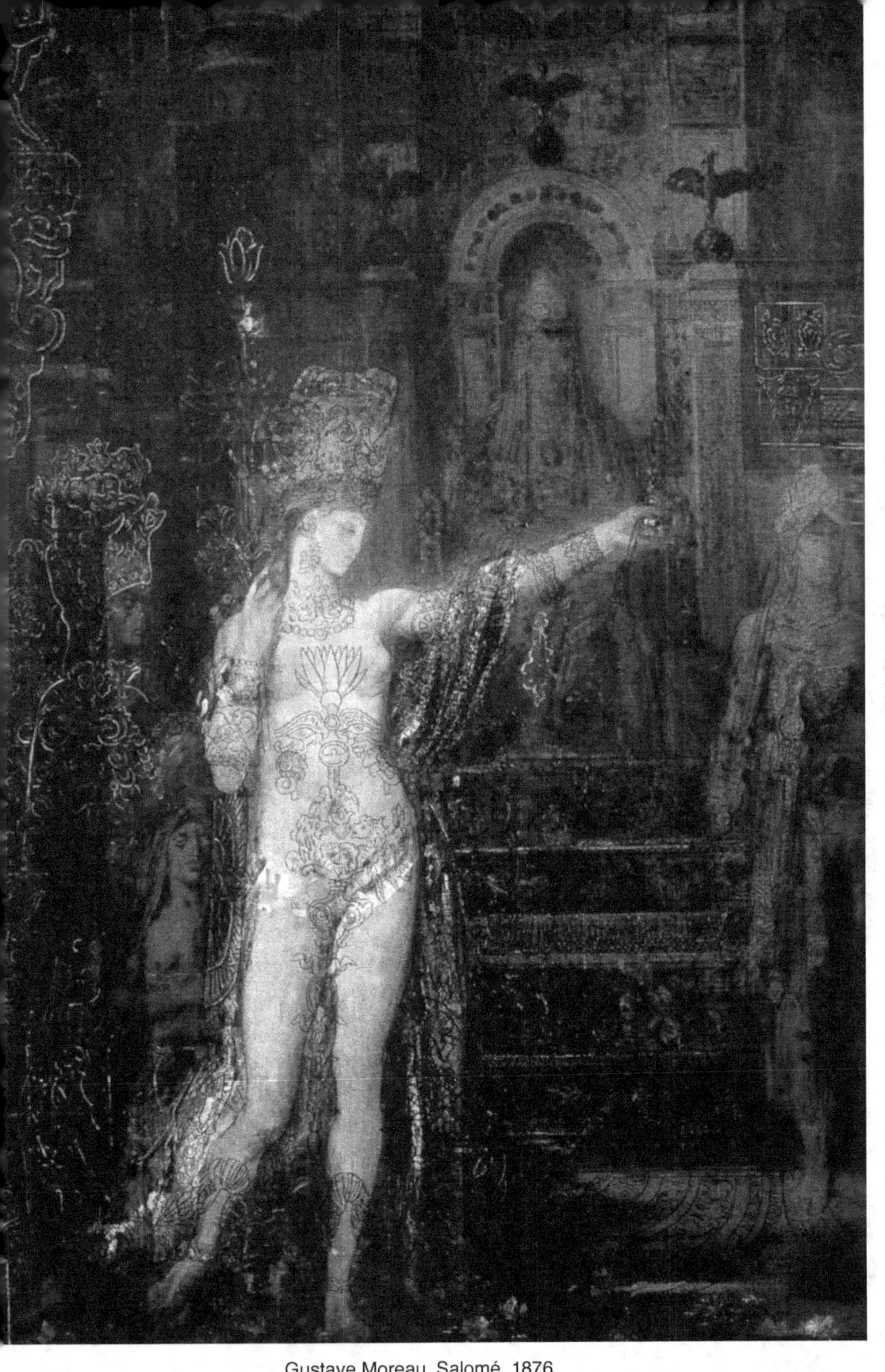

Gustave Moreau, Salomé, 1876

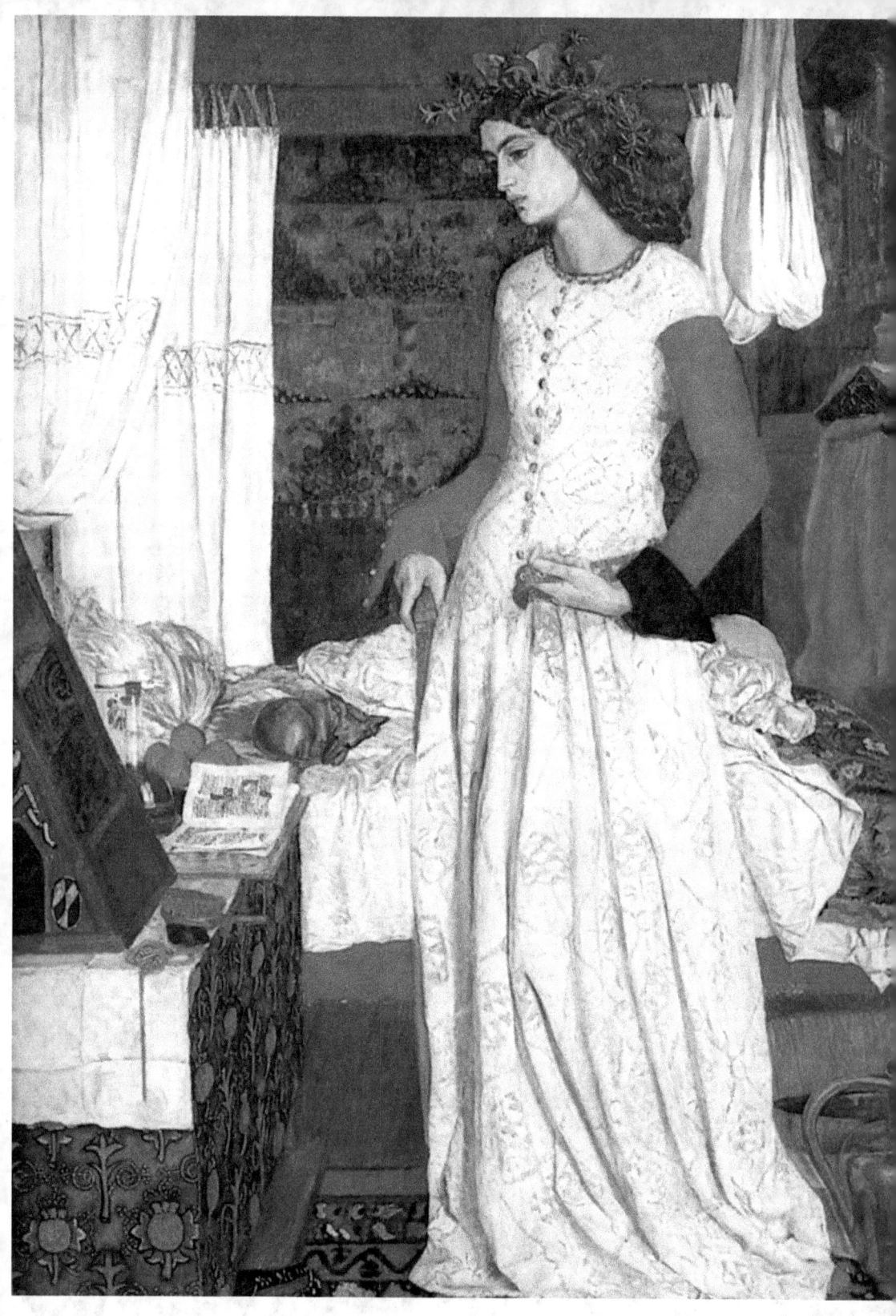

William Morris, La Belle Iseult, 1858, Tate Gallery

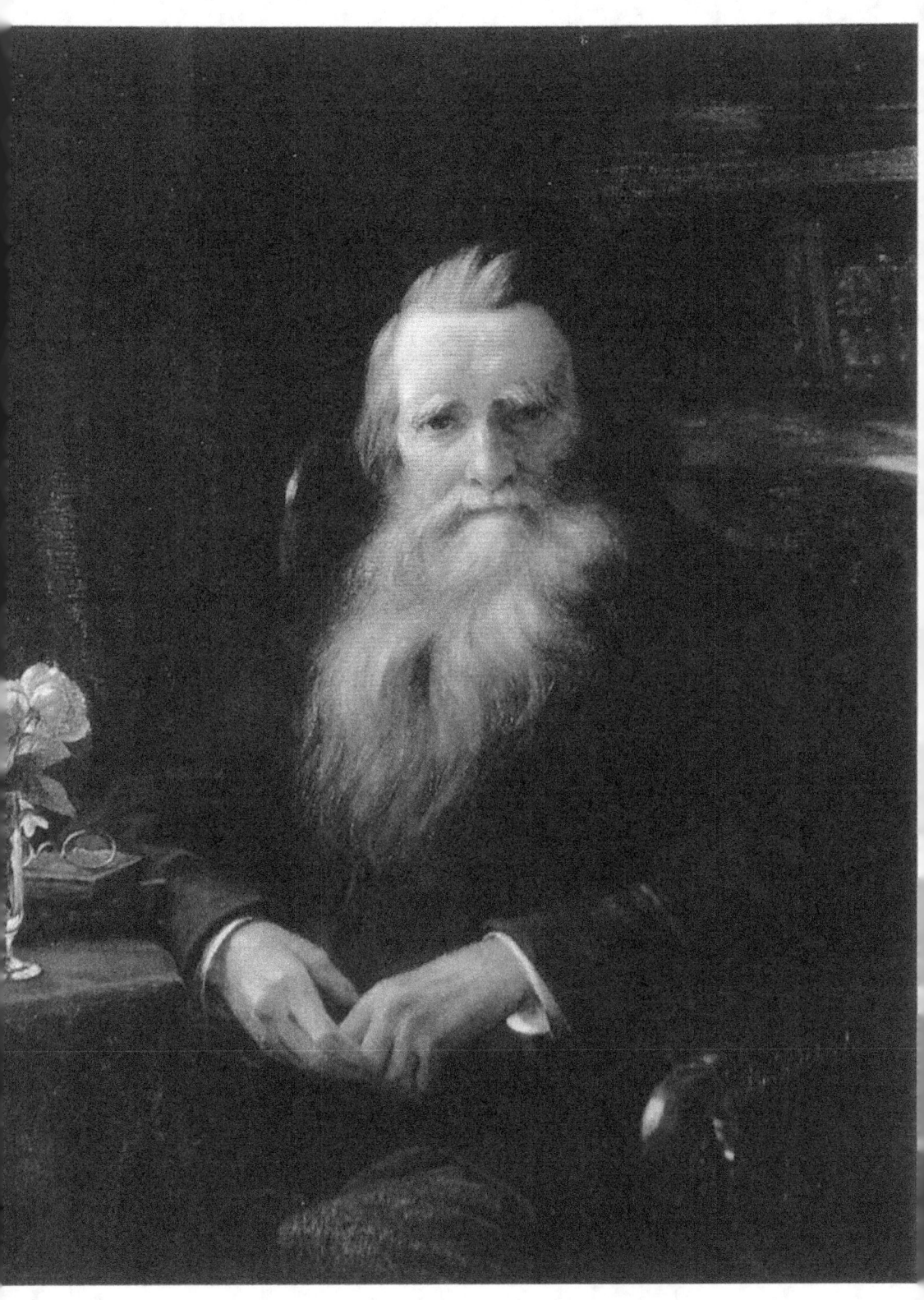

W.G. Collingwood, John Ruskin, 1897

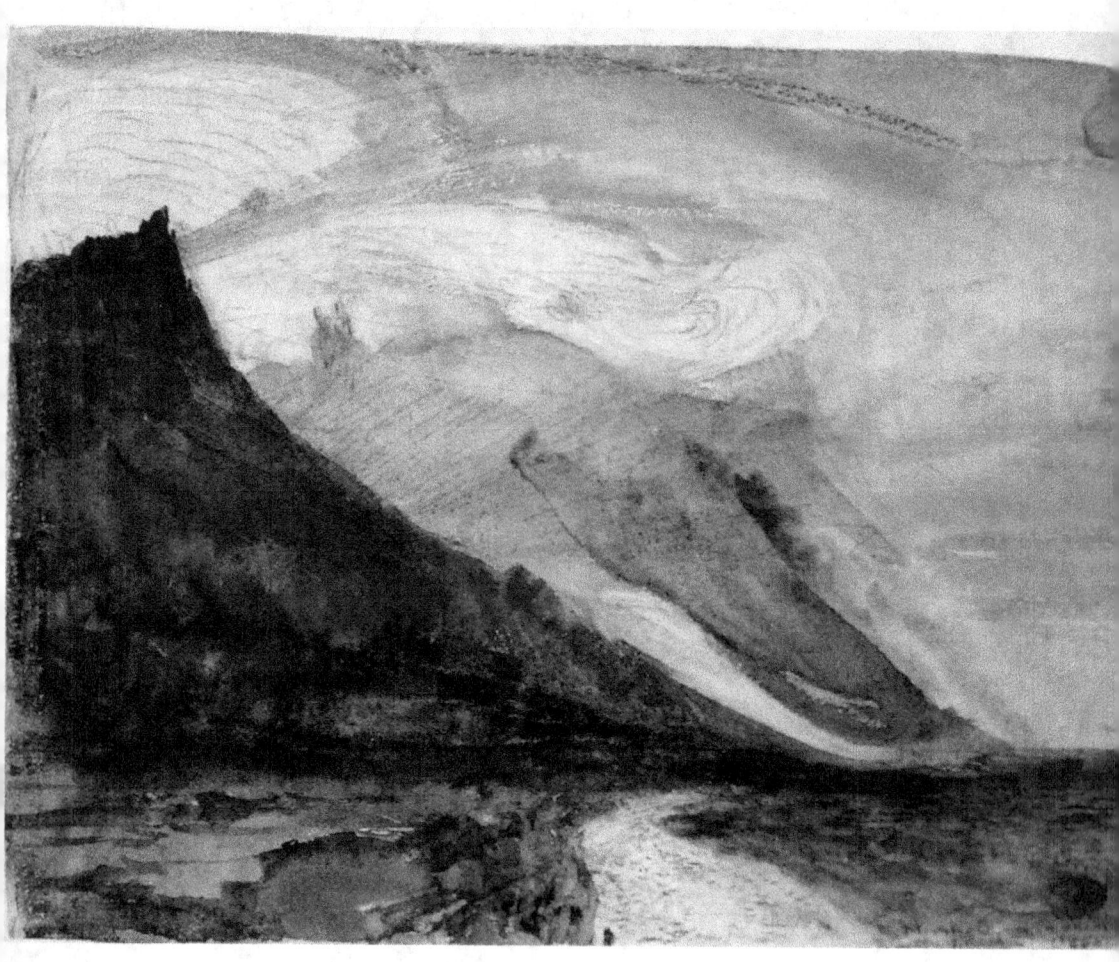

John Ruskin, Moonlight, Chamonix, 1888

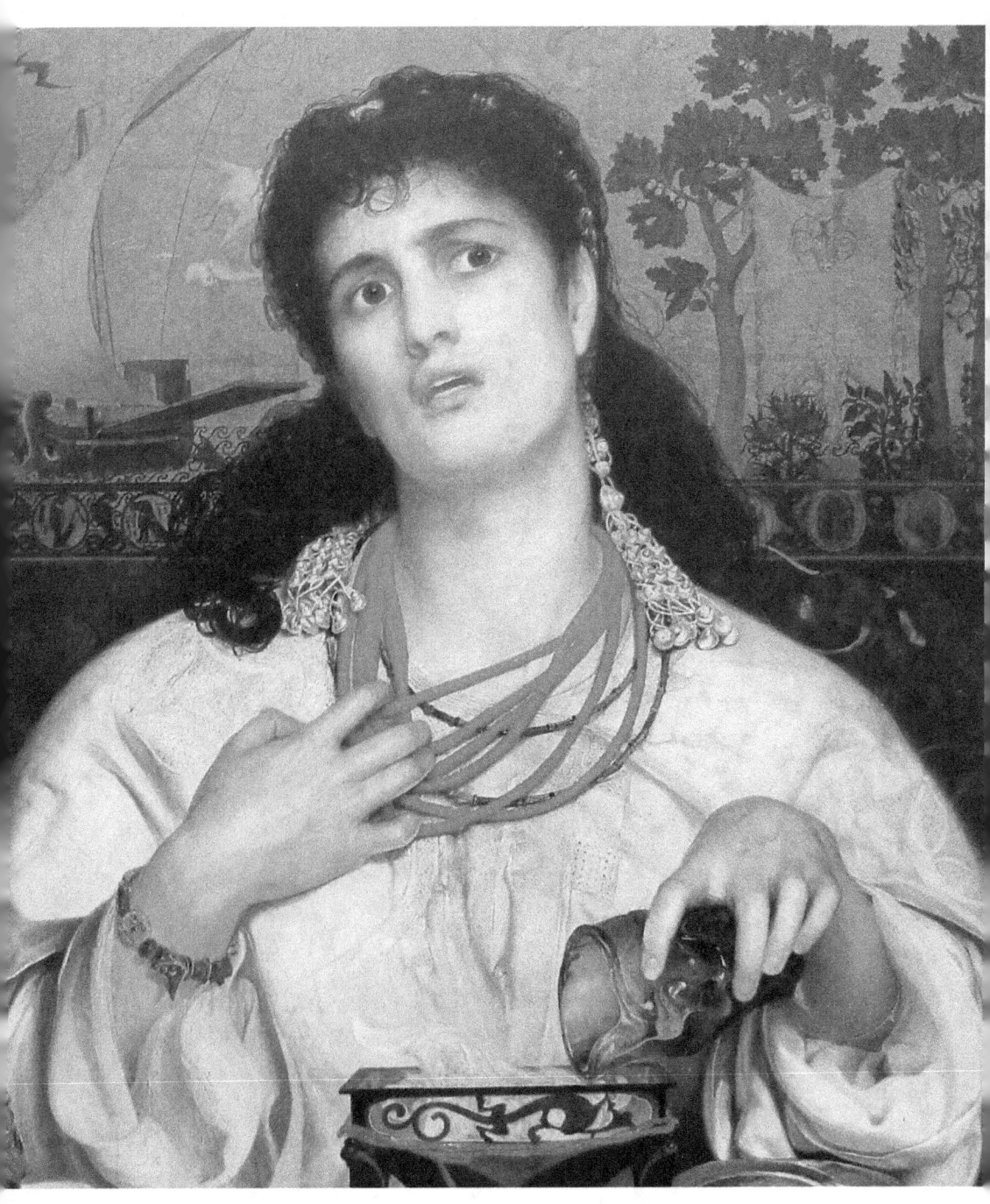

Frederick Sandys, Medea, 1868

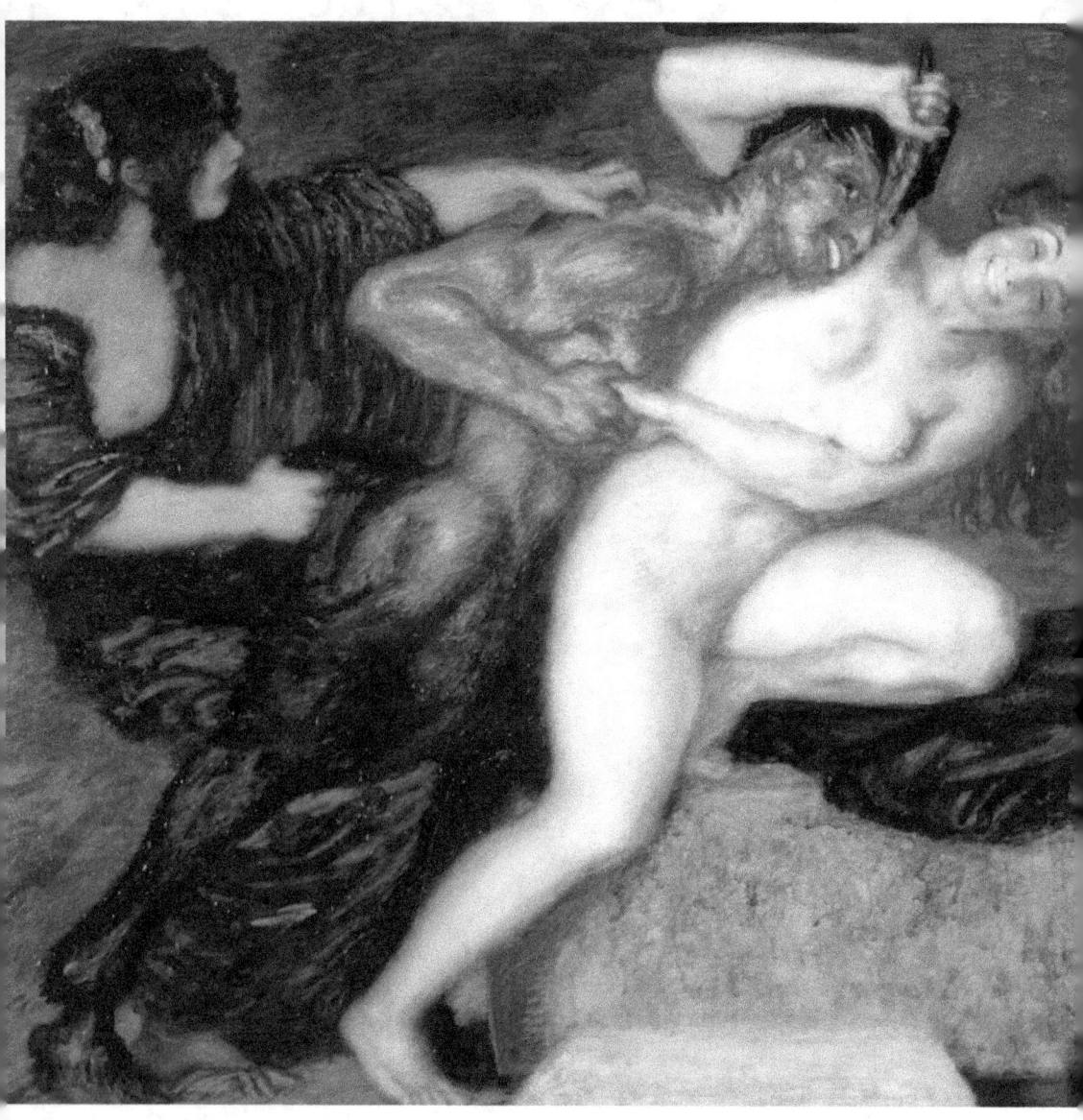

Franz von Stuck, Scherzo

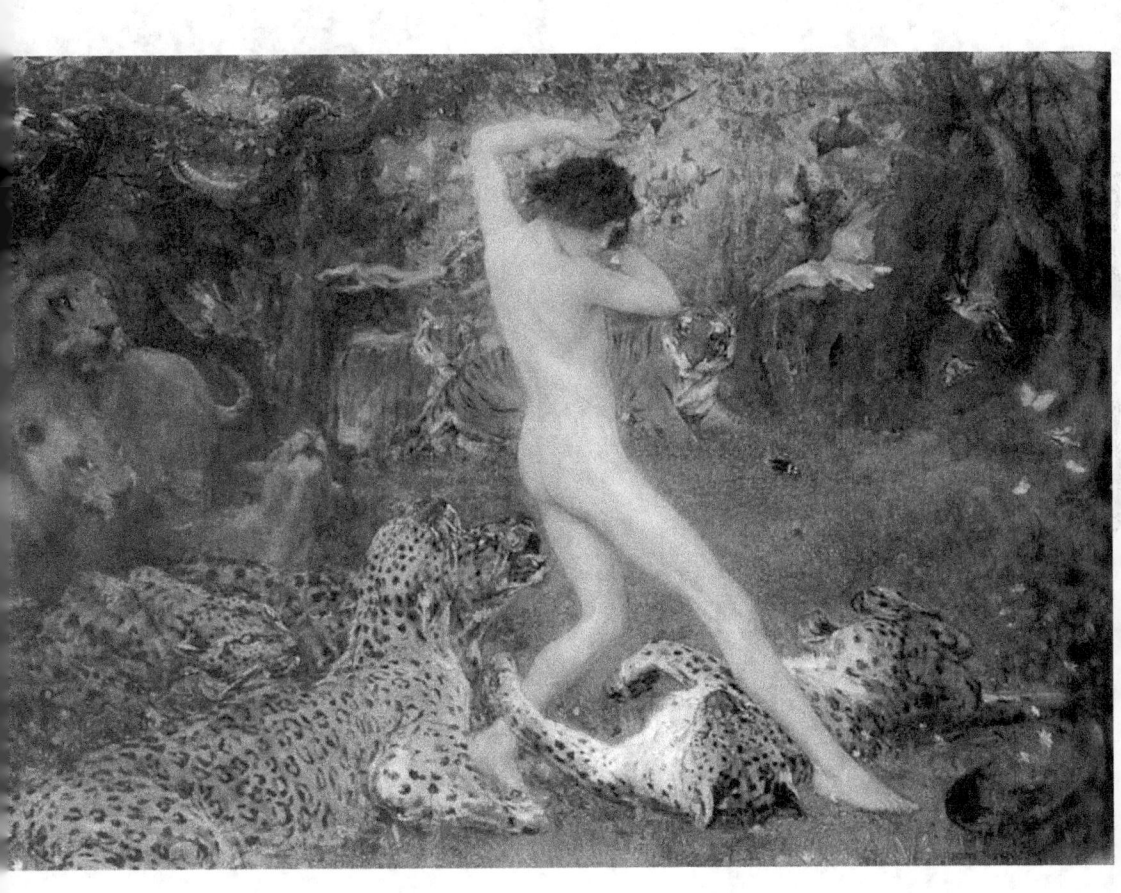

John Macallan Swan, Orpheus, 1896

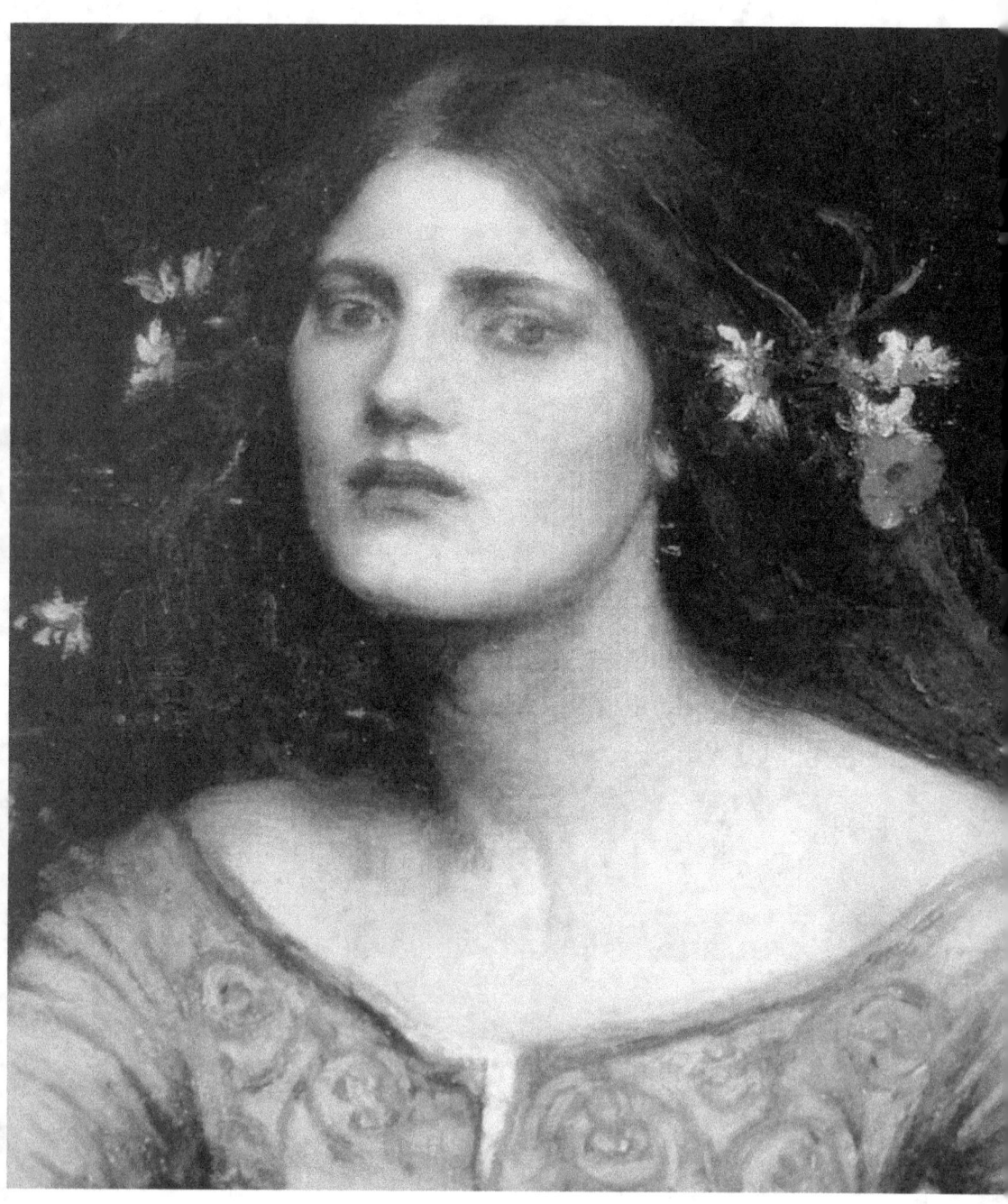

John William Waterhouse, Ophelia, 1910, detail

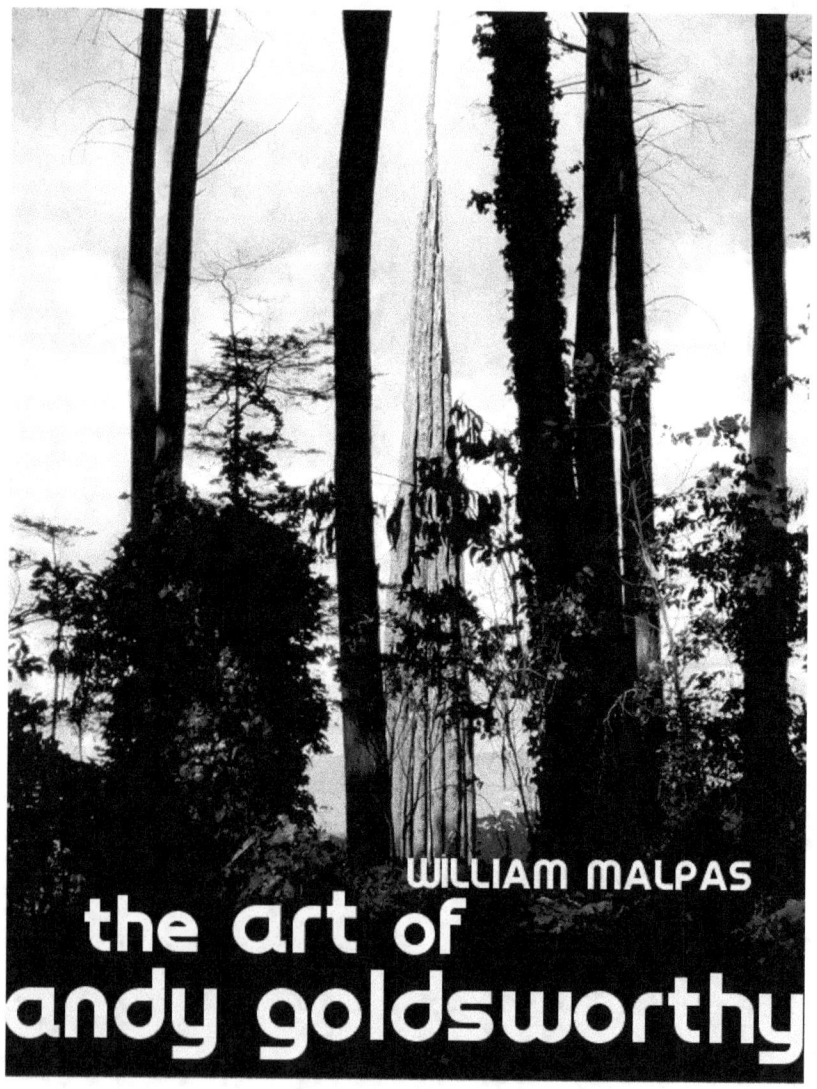

WILLIAM MALPAS
the art of
andy goldsworthy

This is the most comprehensive and detailed account of the art of Andy Goldsworthy available.

This study of Andy Goldsworthy discusses all of Goldsworthy's major exhibitions, books and projects, including the *Sheepfolds* project; *Garden of Stones* in New York; TV and dance collaborations; and the books *Wood, Stone, Time* and *Passage*. William Malpas surveys all of Goldsworthy's output, and analyzes his relation with other land artists such as Robert Smithson, the Christos, Walter de Maria, Chris Drury, Richard Long and David Nash; women sculptors; sculpture in the modern era; and Goldsworthy's place in the contemporary British art scene.

The book has been updated and revised for this new edition.

ISBN 9781861714107 Pbk   ISBN 9781861714114 Hbk
Fully illustrated   www.crmoon.com

Beauties, Beasts, and Enchantment

CLASSIC FRENCH FAIRY TALES

Translated and with an Introduction
by Jack Zipes

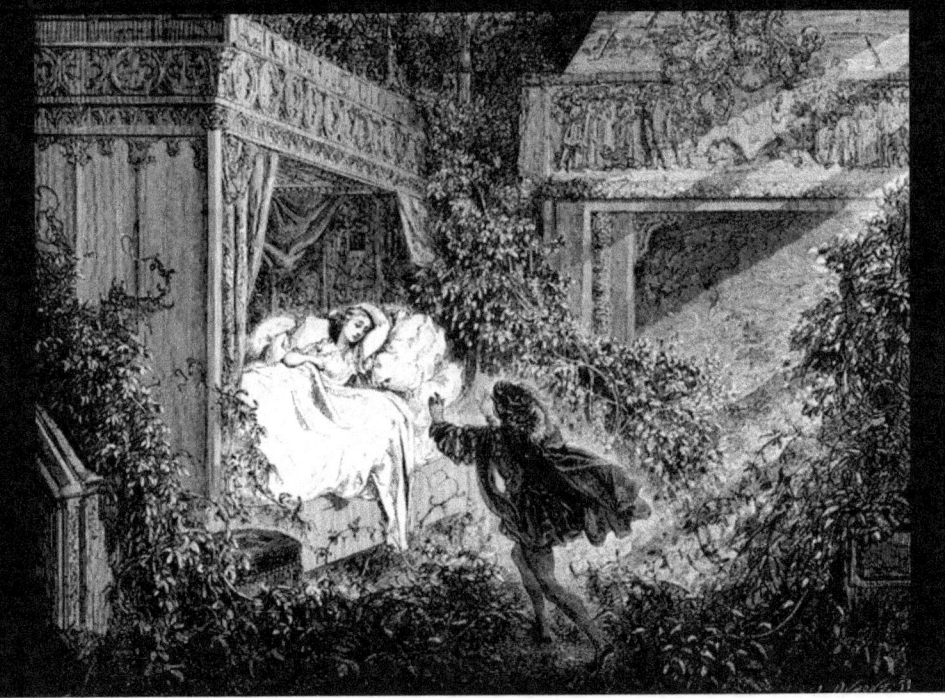

A collection of 36 classic French fairy tales translated by renowned writer Jack Zipes.
Cinderella, Beauty and the Beast, Sleeping Beauty and *Little Red Riding Hood* are among the
classic fairy tales in this amazing book.
Includes illustrations from fairy tale collections.
Jack Zipes has written and published widely on fairy tales.

'Terrific... a succulent array of 17th and 18th century 'salon' fairy tales'
- *The New York Times Book Review*

'These tales are adventurous, thrilling in a way fairy tales are meant to be... The translation
from the French is modern, happily free of archaic and hyperbolic language... a fine and
sophisticated collection' - *New York Tribune*

'Enjoyable to read... a unique collection of French regional folklore' - *Library Journal*

'Charming stories accompanied by attractive pen-and-ink drawings' - *Chattanooga Times*

Introduction and illustrations   612pp.   ISBN 9781861712510 Pbk   ISBN 9781861713193 Hbk

MAURICE SENDAK

& the art of children's book illustration

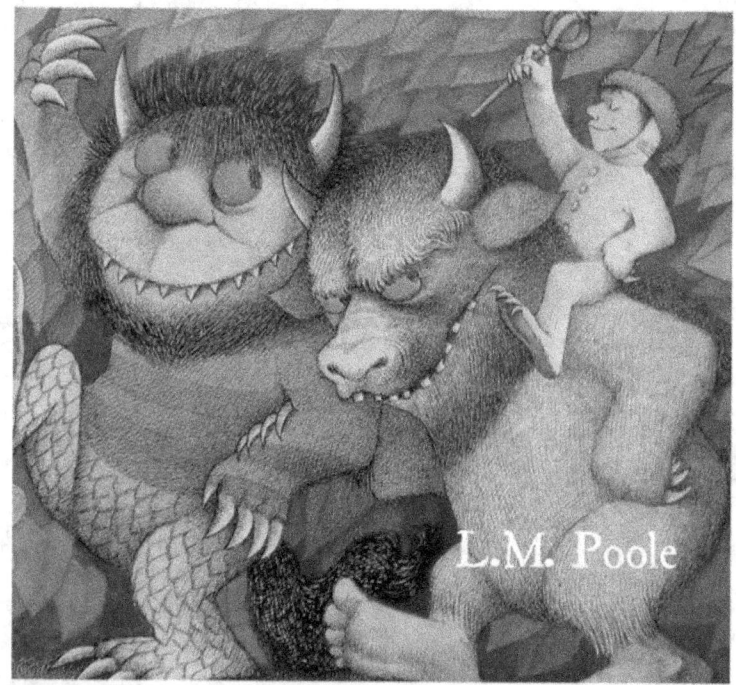

L.M. Poole

Maurice Sendak is the widely acclaimed American children's book author and illustrator. This critical study focuses on his famous trilogy, *Where the Wild Things Are*, *In the Night Kitchen* and *Outside Over There*, as well as the early works and Sendak's superb depictions of the Grimm Brothers' fairy tales in *The Juniper Tree*. L.M. Poole begins with a chapter on children's book illustration, in particular the treatment of fairy tales. Sendak's work is situated within the history of children's book illustration, and he is compared with many contemporary authors.

Fully illustrated. The book has been revised and updated for this edition.
ISBN 9781861714282 Pbk   ISBN 9781861713469 Hbk

CRESCENT MOON PUBLISHING

web: www.crmoon.com e-mail: cresmopub@yahoo.co.uk

ARTS, PAINTING, SCULPTURE

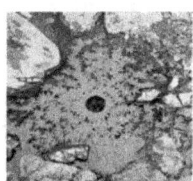

The Art of Andy Goldsworthy
Andy Goldsworthy: Touching Nature
Andy Goldsworthy in Close-Up
Andy Goldsworthy: Pocket Guide
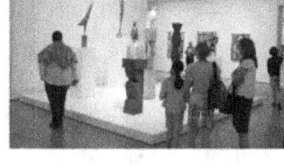
Andy Goldsworthy In America
Land Art: A Complete Guide
The Art of Richard Long
Richard Long: Pocket Guide
Land Art In the UK
Land Art in Close-Up
Land Art In the U.S.A.
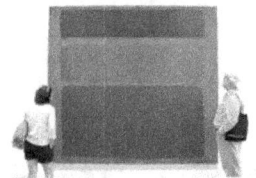
Land Art: Pocket Guide
Installation Art in Close-Up
Minimal Art and Artists In the 1960s and After
Colourfield Painting
Land Art DVD, TV documentary
Andy Goldsworthy DVD, TV documentary
The Erotic Object: Sexuality in Sculpture From Prehistory to the Present Day
Sex in Art: Pornography and Pleasure in Painting and Sculpture
Postwar Art
Sacred Gardens: The Garden in Myth, Religion and Art
Glorification: Religious Abstraction in Renaissance and 20th Century Art
Early Netherlandish Painting
Leonardo da Vinci
Piero della Francesca
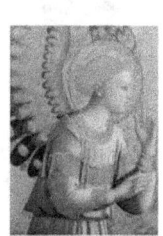
Giovanni Bellini
Fra Angelico: Art and Religion in the Renaissance
Mark Rothko: The Art of Transcendence
Frank Stella: American Abstract Artist
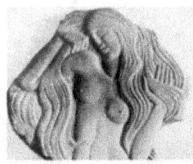
Jasper Johns
Brice Marden
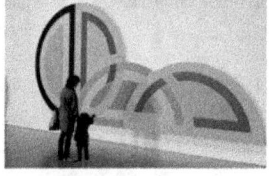
Alison Wilding: The Embrace of Sculpture
Vincent van Gogh: Visionary Landscapes
Eric Gill: Nuptials of God
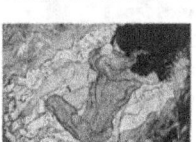
Constantin Brancusi: Sculpting the Essence of Things
Max Beckmann
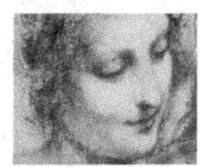
Caravaggio
Gustave Moreau
Egon Schiele: Sex and Death In Purple Stockings
Delizioso Fotografico Fervore: Works In Process 1
Sacro Cuore: Works In Process 2
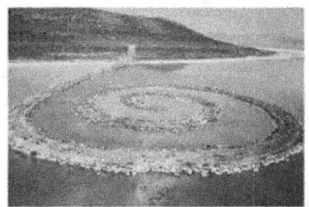
The Light Eternal: J.M.W. Turner
The Madonna Glorified: Karen Arthurs

LITERATURE

J.R.R. Tolkien: The Books, The Films, The Whole Cultural Phenomenon
J.R.R. Tolkien: Pocket Guide
Tolkien's Heroic Quest
The *Earthsea* Books of Ursula Le Guin
Beauties, Beasts and Enchantment: Classic French Fairy Tales
German Popular Stories by the Brothers Grimm
Philip Pullman and *His Dark Materials*
Sexing Hardy: Thomas Hardy and Feminism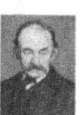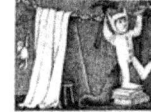
Thomas Hardy's *Tess of the d'Urbervilles*
Thomas Hardy's *Jude the Obscure*
Thomas Hardy: The Tragic Novels
Love and Tragedy: Thomas Hardy
The Poetry of Landscape in Hardy
Wessex Revisited: Thomas Hardy and John Cowper Powys
Wolfgang Iser: Essays and Interviews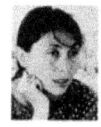
Petrarch, Dante and the Troubadours
Maurice Sendak and the Art of Children's Book Illustration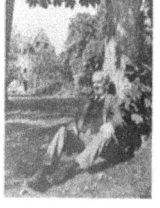
Andrea Dworkin
Cixous, Irigaray, Kristeva: The *Jouissance* of French Feminism
Julia Kristeva: Art, Love, Melancholy, Philosophy, Semiotics and Psychoanalysis
Hélene Cixous I Love You: The *Jouissance* of Writing
Luce Irigaray: Lips, Kissing, and the Politics of Sexual Difference
Peter Redgrove: Here Comes the Flood
Peter Redgrove: Sex-Magic-Poetry-Cornwall
Lawrence Durrell: Between Love and Death, East and West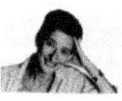
Love, Culture & Poetry: Lawrence Durrell
Cavafy: Anatomy of a Soul
German Romantic Poetry: Goethe, Novalis, Heine, Hölderlin
Feminism and Shakespeare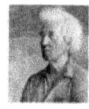
Shakespeare: Love, Poetry & Magic
The Passion of D.H. Lawrence
D.H. Lawrence: Symbolic Landscapes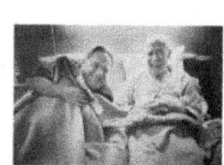
D.H. Lawrence: Infinite Sensual Violence
Rimbaud: Arthur Rimbaud and the Magic of Poetry
The Ecstasies of John Cowper Powys
Sensualism and Mythology: The Wessex Novels of John Cowper Powys
Amorous Life: John Cowper Powys and the Manifestation of Affectivity (H.W. Fawkner)
Postmodern Powys: New Essays on John Cowper Powys (Joe Boulter)
Rethinking Powys: Critical Essays on John Cowper Powys
Paul Bowles & Bernardo Bertolucci
Rainer Maria Rilke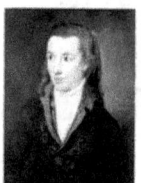
Joseph Conrad: *Heart of Darkness*
In the Dim Void: Samuel Beckett
Samuel Beckett Goes into the Silence
André Gide: Fiction and Fervour
Jackie Collins and the Blockbuster Novel
Blinded By Her Light: The Love-Poetry of Robert Graves
The Passion of Colours: Travels In Mediterranean Lands
Poetic Forms

POETRY

Ursula Le Guin: Walking In Cornwall
Peter Redgrove: Here Comes The Flood
Peter Redgrove: Sex-Magic-Poetry-Cornwall
Dante: Selections From the Vita Nuova
Petrarch, Dante and the Troubadours
William Shakespeare: Sonnets
William Shakespeare: Complete Poems
Blinded By Her Light: The Love-Poetry of Robert Graves
Emily Dickinson: Selected Poems
Emily Brontë: Poems
Thomas Hardy: Selected Poems
Percy Bysshe Shelley: Poems
John Keats: Selected Poems
Joh n Keats: Poems of 1820
D.H. Lawrence: Selected Poems
Edmund Spenser: Poems
Edmund Spenser: Amoretti
John Donne: Poems
Henry Vaughan: Poems
Sir Thomas Wyatt: Poems
Robert Herrick: Selected Poems
Rilke: Space, Essence and Angels in the Poetry of Rainer Maria Rilke
Rainer Maria Rilke: Selected Poems
Friedrich Hölderlin: Selected Poems
Arseny Tarkovsky: Selected Poems
Arthur Rimbaud: Selected Poems
Arthur Rimbaud: A Season in Hell
Arthur Rimbaud and the Magic of Poetry
Novalis: Hymns To the Night
German Romantic Poetry
Paul Verlaine: Selected Poems
Elizaethan Sonnet Cycles
D.J. Enright: By-Blows
Jeremy Reed: Brigitte's Blue Heart
Jeremy Reed: Claudia Schiffer's Red Shoes
Gorgeous Little Orpheus
Radiance: New Poems
Crescent Moon Book of Nature Poetry
Crescent Moon Book of Love Poetry
Crescent Moon Book of Mystical Poetry
Crescent Moon Book of Elizabethan Love Poetry
Crescent Moon Book of Metaphysical Poetry
Crescent Moon Book of Romantic Poetry
Pagan America: New American Poetry

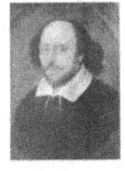
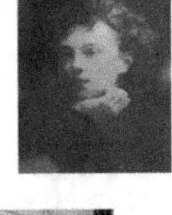
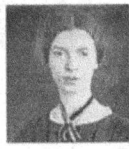
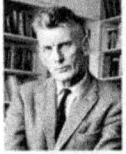
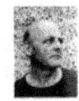
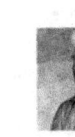
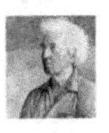
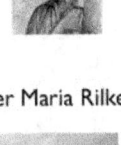
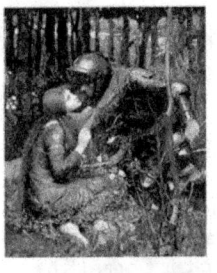
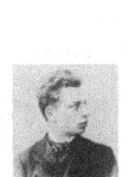
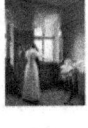
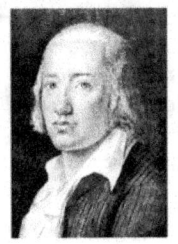
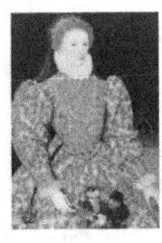

J.R.R. Tolkien: The Books, The Films, The Whole Cultural Phenomenon
J.R.R. Tolkien: Pocket Guide
The *Lord of the Rings* Movies: Pocket Guide
The Cinema of Hayao Miyazaki
Hayao Miyazaki: *Princess Mononoke*: Pocket Movie Guide
Hayao Miyazaki: *Spirited Away*: Pocket Movie Guide
Tim Burton : Hallowe'en For Hollywood
Ken Russell
Ken Russell: *Tommy*: Pocket Movie Guide
The Ghost Dance: The Origins of Religion
The Peyote Cult
Cixous, Irigaray, Kristeva: The *Jouissance* of French Feminism
Julia Kristeva: Art, Love, Melancholy, Philosophy, Semiotics and Psychoanalysis
Luce Irigaray: Lips, Kissing, and the Politics of Sexual Difference
Hélene Cixous I Love You: The *Jouissance* of Writing
Andrea Dworkin
'Cosmo Woman': The World of Women's Magazines
Women in Pop Music
HomeGround: The Kate Bush Anthology
Discovering the Goddess (Geoffrey Ashe)
The Poetry of Cinema
The Sacred Cinema of Andrei Tarkovsky
Andrei Tarkovsky: Pocket Guide
Andrei Tarkovsky: *Mirror*: Pocket Movie Guide
Andrei Tarkovsky: *The Sacrifice*: Pocket Movie Guide
Walerian Borowczyk: Cinema of Erotic Dreams
Jean-Luc Godard: The Passion of Cinema
Jean-Luc Godard: *Hail Mary*: Pocket Movie Guide
Jean-Luc Godard: *Contempt*: Pocket Movie Guide
Jean-Luc Godard: *Pierrot le Fou*: Pocket Movie Guide
John Hughes and Eighties Cinema
Ferris Bueller's Day Off: Pocket Movie Guide
Jean-Luc Godard: Pocket Guide
The Cinema of Richard Linklater
Liv Tyler: Star In Ascendance
Blade Runner and the Films of Philip K. Dick
Paul Bowles and Bernardo Bertolucci
Media Hell: Radio, TV and the Press
An Open Letter to the BBC
Detonation Britain: Nuclear War in the UK
Feminism and Shakespeare
Wild Zones: Pornography, Art and Feminism
Sex in Art: Pornography and Pleasure in Painting and Sculpture
Sexing Hardy: Thomas Hardy and Feminism

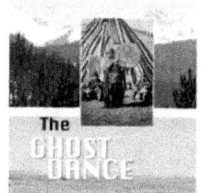
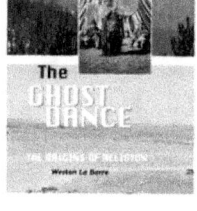
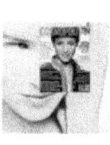
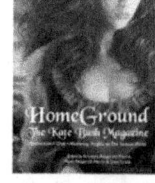
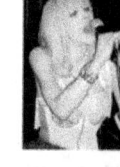
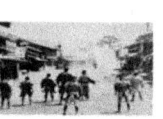
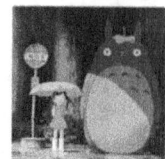
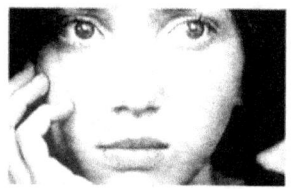

The Light Eternal is a model monograph, an exemplary job. The subject matter of the book is beautifully organised and dead on beam. (Lawrence Durrell)
It is amazing for me to see my work treated with such passion and respect. (Andrea Dworkin)

CRESCENT MOON PUBLISHING
P.O. Box 1312, Maidstone, Kent, ME14 5XU, Great Britain. www.crmoon.com

cresmopub@yahoo.co.uk   www.crescentmoon.org.uk